Cannibals

A children's story about eating cannibals !!

I was struck on one of the sites of foreign analysis, the literary-historical history of Germany is old and famous all over the world, it is a funny story for children, but it contains the terrible truth about the chapters of the grotesque from the history of mankind, you rarely wait and wait, when, and you reminded me My grandmother, God rest her soul, who had a habit of picking up leftover bread from the dinner table and drying it safe and sound in a big bag under the bed of a brass old lady, and when we laughed at who did it, she shook her head and answered innovatively: " you have a right to it. " laugh, you are not hungry. "Come with me, dear readers, along with a piece of the dark and forgotten history of generations of mankind.

The story of Hans and Gretel

Probably most of us have read or heard, or even saw on TV the story of Hans and Greta, which does not allow for a quick review. No, Hans and Gretel's story was published in a collection of stories for children in Germany in 1812 and is about a boy and a girl, their father was the lumberjack is too poor, but because he cannot give his son food for the family and asked his wife (sometimes she appears to be the wife of her father, and sometimes to another mother Real) I take the children to the forest and leave them there, fortunately, we, the children heard the plan of their father's wife (or their mother), so they decided to collect a white stone and throw it behind them while their father walks with them into the forest to take it with him. At home, when they leave their father in the forest, and the queue of the kids has already changed after the father disappeared and left them alone. They watched the Gravel, which scattered them and was able to return them home, But after a while it became more difficult to put the parents and there was no food, you cannot even feed the family, so his wife again asked the children to go to the forest and leave them there, and onthis time I also heard the children that he intends to their father, they repeat their plan, but this time they did not give them time to collect pebbles, so they use small pieces of bread to soak it behind them, and unfortunately for them I ate birds and animals cut bread, so I did not listen to the children at home and got lost in the forest until they came into the house with darkness, everything was made of candies and sugar was cut so that they took them from the walls and windows until I got out of the old hag and did not ask them to come into the house for more milk. And the fact that I came to the house until they discovered that the old witch was deceiving the little ones with sweets to stop and eat them, and the old lock witch was even fattened to eat, and Greta was used as a servant, and on the day when I decided to cook and eat asked Greta to go into the oven to make sure everything is ready for the barbecue, and other tricks the old woman and convince her that the interference with the oven and what I did so close the oven doors and freed her brother escaped on Monday from the witch's house after he stole her jewelry and returned to his father's house to live a happy and carefree life after that, and the story ended.

The roots of the present before
The Middle Ages knew many areas and it happened where there are many bad things that turned some people into monsters and people do not know mercy, it is human nature and the instinct for survival, the lives of millions of people in the world were obtained And even in the days of prosperity, the majority of the population lived in conditions extreme poverty, so it rarely happens that a person is asleep and full of belly and it is not unusual to see many homeless children on the streets at that time, who died, their parents, the average age of a person in the Middle Ages does not exceed at best 40 years , and this percentage falls during the war and plague until the age of 18, and it was not wondrous during the reign of the parents of their children to think over their own food on their own or just die away from their eyes, and this was the best place to attack outside the city or villages in the wild or in the forest, so they cannot go home and not find someone helping them on Go back to the house, there were children starving to death or preyed animals, and it rarely happens that someone finds them and

rescues them. During the reign, and when you reach a climax, so there is nothing to eat, and when you take weeds, wild and leaves, mice and insects, there will be no choice but to feed on human flesh, yes dear readers, people become food for humans, - it is not cruel as it is an instinct to survive, in Europe and in one of the regions, talks about the disagreements between two women, and the reason is that both agreed to eat their children and decided to see ate children and the next time to eat Children. others, and had already managed to slaughter and boil and eat children, women, and when he came to himself so that the second woman would refuse to kill and eat her children, perhaps laugh, dear readers, and you think that this is a myth, but stories like this , occurred in the districts, and similar atrocities may occur in the last and best free mainstream known to the Arabs on Mount Lebanon in 1919, when the bodies lit up the streets and alleys of Beirut and people hid their children for fear of kidnapping, and there is so talk of cannibalism, because of the famine in Ukraine in the 1930s, as well as United Nations reports, turns to cannibalism because of the famine in North Korea between 1995-1997. So there are people in the districts, this is not uncommon, and the author of the story about Hans and Gretel is inspired by the story of this bloody story, this is a funny story for children, but in fact the controller for a terrible fact happened and repeated itself through the entire history of the districts long ago, in the field of the next the year 1065 and which lasted seven years, became the price of a loaf of bread 15 dinars in gold and trade historians have many stories of cannibalism, and in Europe in 1317 he became a normal cannibal and stole children in order to kill them and eat them, and was often carried out by women to trick children, lure them and kidnap them, and is documented by historians who have written many such stories of gangs robbing people and children. Especially for food, and this is because it is easy for children to deceive and silence them, so the old woman in the tale of Hans and Gretel is not a fictional character, but at heart it is true, and the story as a whole is inspired by the fact that the fathers of their children are abandoned. for poverty and hunger, to deceive and rob children and eat them. and everyone knows that the easiest way to deceive a child is about the same to seduce him with candy. And the more we remember when we were children, how our parents warned us about strangers and how they disappointed us sometimes with a game or an evil witch who will tell us and will eat us if we do not calm down or fall asleep, and that our parents did not see an evil witch or an evil witch in their lives, but heard her from their parents

The strangest case of cannibalism

The crime of the wondrous has puzzled the world not with its ugliness, but, oddly enough, also with the fact that being a victim in this crime is even crazier and more cruel than the template itself, so that investigators have to choose who is the culprit in this heinous crime - the victim or the murderer.
The crime of a wonderfully perplexed world is not its ugliness, but, oddly enough, also in order to be the victim of this crime is even more insane and cruel than the template itself, so investigators

need to choose which of them is guilty of this disgusting the crime of the victim or murderer.

Crime hero German Armin Miffia "Armin Mezhvids" born in 1961, and what works of art for computers and who put this ad online curious "we need to structure the person between 18-30 age before slaughter and devour" and it is strange that Armin found a volunteer for this a request and an architect from Germany named Bernd Brendang, 43, and a freak and pedophile, and had the two met in March 2001, where Brand's Armenian lobby went to his house and saw that the room would kill him and cut him out and then swallow the brands a huge number of pills and painkillers, and in Armenia they killed him, ate parts of his body and filmed the crime on film - all this for two hours.

At the very beginning (according to one journalist who managed to see the tape at a closed hearing in court, where it is shown to the public), the request of Brand Armenia B says to cut off his penis by biting with his teeth, and does not deny this, did Armin cut it open with a knife and made part of it to a brand to eat. but the latter could not eat my share of his penis, although he was lucky in his mouth and it crushed a severe trauma as a result of the loss of a lot of blood, said Armin, put the penis in a saucepan and added salt, pepper and a little garlic and it was, and but the latter became very weak as a result of bleeding, despite the fact that Armin gave him plenty of drinks and pain relievers. He told Armin, giving him bleeding in the bathroom for several hours, and then he arranged to drag him to his room in his house for this purpose and it was to cut his throat from his neck and hung the organs of the butcher's inverter and he cut the amount of meat (about ten kilograms) to store it in the refrigerator and continued to eat them for several months. Captured by Armenia in December 2002 after I posted another ad on the internet (when the boat was in full force), requesting a new victim, said that the investigators were following him and they searched his house, they found parts of the victim's hull of his previous brands But the court recognized the problem of Armenia's guilt, namely because there were no materials legally condemning cannibalism in Germany, and we do not have murder on the grounds that the victim voluntarily agreed to be killed, since he partially participated in the murder process and chomping (it was beneficial for Armenia to have an accomplice in the crime in order to prove that the murder was committed by mutual consent and at the request of the victim himself), but the charge threatens Armin with charges of murder for sexual pleasure and violation of the immunity of the deceased, and for the Armenian government, to put Miev in prison for eight and a half years.

And in 2006, Armin was tried again because of the ugliness of his crime and terror and panic caused by the beam of general well-being of the victim.Hum Brands (according to the prosecution) suffered from sexual and mental disorders and was addicted to alcoholic beverages and drugs fast loading of Armin store disorders the victim and the regiment he killed to the Armenian Miffy on charges of murder and was convicted and sentenced to life imprisonment (the death penalty was abolished in Germany).

In fact, I from conversations between the two through one of the online forums show that Brandis's victim was impatient and agitated to kill him and ate (maybe even more than in the next Armenia) in the first messages exchanged between them tell Armin that he prepares meat for dinner and he replies to Brandis stating: (you don't need to buy meat after today, there will be many).

And in another letter I am surprised at brands: (what will you do with my brain?) He Armin: (I'm going to leave him because I don't want to break your skull) brands: (I'd rather pay for this in an article or maybe you have to pull it) should drag Armenia in favor: (there is a small graveyard and quite close to my house), but the brands back offer it, saying: (you can use it one car).

And in another letter, he says brands are on offer: (I hope you are serious because I really want to do this) and then ask: (do you smoke?) He Armin: (yes, but my teeth are still whiter, than whites) then brands sarcastically: (that's good because I smoked too, I hope you enjoy the taste of smoked meat).

And plus brands, there are about 200 people who wrote to Armin in response to his statement, perhaps some kind of joke, but Armin said in court that he met five of them and brought them to his house to go and meet them, but they retreated at the last moment, which of the things the Armenian mentioned to protect himself, where he said that one of the volunteers asked me to teach in the same chalkboard, and then skin him like a pig. and we, maybe, to one of the nearest ones after work and hung it on the inverter, but retreated at the last moment, left it after I hung out a little and we drank a few glasses of beer and ate pizza ..

In fact, Armenia Miffy was a psychopath psychologically, where he thought that his father's preference for his youngest caused his psychological complex and imagined from childhood that he would kill his younger brother. or his schoolmates, and devoured their bodies, and said that the horror films I watched as a child stimulated his desire to kill people and devour them, and just told Armin in court (that he had fantasies .... back to reality) he intends to write a book about his experience of cannibalism, as he believes that there are about 800 cannibals in Germany, and also insists on having thousands of people who are hungry, but they are unlucky because they are not can find anyone to eat them. (not the case, according to him) when he said, as we mentioned earlier, that five people responded to the declaration he published on the Internet, but he did not find in them the qualities they are looking for.

After in the case of Armenia, dozens of sites have appeared on the Internet, the cannibals are looking for people for problems and can be commented on by Armenia saying: (they cannot do the same quality as you !!).

Sony Bean and his violent family

The story of Sauna Mezh and his family is expected from a famous story in Scotland and revolves around a family who disappeared in one of the caves on the coast of Scotland for a quarter of a century was the source of her life only during this period is human meat for unfortunate travelers who passed this region photos of the family and committed them, and although some doubt the origin of the history of the sauna in the meantime, there are others who confirm their appearance and in all cases offer you, dear reader, a complete story for the average family.

Boy sauna in between ((Sony Bean In the Scottish countryside a few miles east of the city of Edinburgh during the time of King James the First, King of Scotland, his father worked in fencing farms and set his son to pursue the same career, in his youth was a sauna between receiving a piece of bread, working with my father, but he was predisposed to laziness and comfort, so I did not want to develop his work and continue it, but left my father and mother and fled to the countryside far away with a woman, no less in a dressing gown and salad.

This Monday he settled in one of the caves off the coast of the countryside in Galway, where he lived for twenty-five years, without visiting a single village or city, without trading in women.

And over time, it became, they have many children and grandchildren who were brought up in the same way as they were isolated from people and were not called a single person, and lived all these years, kidnapping people, and they were so cruel that they did not leave one a kidnapped person without killing him.

Thanks to this method, the blood and lack of respect for them continued for a long time without being discovered or seen by one, and no one could understand why some people disappear when they pass the area inhabited by the sauna family between them.

So choose a family, an evil person or a woman or a child, to take him to the cave and there they cut him open and devour him, and at night they throw the heads and legs and the remains of their victims to the hunters, helpless at sea and in the area far from the cave. so as not to incur suspicion on them, and these were human remains, carried with water to various beaches of the country, causing horror and bewilderment in the hearts of people.

A large number of people who disappear in the area where Sony and his family live began to raise doubts in the hearts of the people, so they began to send spies and ghosts to the region to discover something, but some of them never returned and disappeared forever, as long as they were lucky and they did not become the prey of the expected family, they did not see anything suspicious.

I began to question the owners of hotels and hostels in these areas because many of the people who disappeared in those areas spent their last night in one of these hostels, and some of the owners of the hostels were arrested and interrogated and tortured to obtain confessions. and some who did the rest were executed, they closed their hotels and theirs and left home for fear of noticing the same source.

These heinous crimes both sowed terror and fear in the Kingdom and many innocent people who were suspected were arrested and executed. But despite all this, a series of disappearances and the emergence of parties of humanity on the beaches continued, prompting many people to leave the area and move to other areas, safer.

Meanwhile, in the family of saunas between her, the number of children and grandchildren was growing through the marriage of brothers of the past, and all this was in the family of those involved in cruel murders, and they were very careful not to be found, they only attacked travelers, and burned less and more wars that not a single person got to them, whether on foot or on horseback, they were surrounded by victims on each side and enclosed them in a circle from which it is impossible to escape or escape from them. And it is the cavemen living just a few meters from the beach and sheltered by trees and water that enter the large space inside the cave with the tide and flood the entrance to the cave so that none of the inspection teams and searchers that have been sent by the state complain. that someone lives in this cave deserted and dark. That the number of victims of this family of evil he never knew, but in general it can be assumed that they killed at least a thousand people men, women and children during the five and twentieth years, when they lived in the cave, and this continued until then, until the day came when one of their victims fled from them.

One day one of the men was returning to his home with his wife and was riding on his horse and suddenly surrounded the demons, the family bath, between them from all sides, but the man put up strong resistance to them and could wound a large number of them with his pistol and sword and in the meantime his wife fell poor because of the horse taking out the cattle and one of the girls of the family of evil cut her throat immediately, and the other disarmed her clothes and directed her womb and cut her, which made her husband in the resistance of the average family, because that he was sure that the same fate awaited him and that he himself managed to hide among the trees of the forest and found behind him twenty or thirty people from the bath family between the bodies of his poor wife expected and walking by them so that his cave would understand this at night. And so, this man, who was the first person who could leave the family, was waiting for news for all people what happened to him, which caused their surprise and their fear, and they took him to the capital of Glasgow to inform the government where immediately sent to the royal court to tell their terrible story.

For three to four days, an armed big march led by the king himself with hundreds of men who set off from the capital in search of the family available, and the only guy who escaped the hands of the family sauna between them leads them, and they may decide not to leave the stone. until they looked underneath, and not just a tree, and they looked behind them, bringing with them at the same time a large number of hunting dogs trained to assist them in the research process.

The search process continues for a long time, without finding any traces or clues leading to the bath between his family and although they passed next to the cave in which he lives, unless he aroused their suspicions and listened to the sea on the beach without success, but when he got off tide and water was discovered, then from the entrance to the cave, a floor number entered and emitted a large burst of barking, which piqued the curiosity of the king, who is usually A and his people and they stopped at the entrance to the cave, not one that someone can live in such a cave, dark and dreary, but at the same time the buzzing of words did not stop and even intensified, as I more and more went inside the cave and did not work. all attempts to bring her back. which raised doubts, the king ordered a large number of people to enter the cave. The DLF King's men infiltrated and infiltrated the cave until they reached the gruesome location that houses the monster family's sauna between them.

I watched the people of the king in a cave that no mind can imagine ... legs ... hands ... human heads ... all men, women and children had rows of dried meat on the walls, huge amounts of human bones were covered the floor, the number of coins, gold, silver, banknotes were stacked on top of each other, along with watches, rings, swords, pistols and a very large amount of clothes and other things, the family had to collect from their helpless victims.

It was a family bath between a medium, consisting of the arrested, besides him and his wife, evil eight boys and six girls and eighteen grandchildren, as well as fourteen great-granddaughters, and they were all the result of a wife, incest between brothers and sisters.

All members of the family of the unclean were arrested and all the human remains found in the cave were burned, the royal people collected all the things they found from money and clothes, and the transferred king galloped back to the capital and already strangled cities and villages, where thousands of people gathered to look at the family a bath among the damned.

Upon the arrival of the king in the capital, the trial of the family did not correspond to anyone, because they did not enjoy only one fate - to die without mercy, as they do with their innocent victims.

For the forest, the men lost me and the rest of the family, they cut their hands and feet and left them to bleed for several hours, as for the women, the villain's wife and her daughters and granddaughters forced them to watch their men being killed, and then collect all and burn them in three separate fires, and even until the last moment of their lives it did not seem that someone from the bath family was between any signs of remorse, it was their cries and their wild curses, it was the rapprochement of heaven with their unfortunate evil spirits.

Al-Jahiz and the Arab cannibals

In the heritage, everyone has stories and news about eating human flesh, some about the campaign of some peoples as part of their daily food or their religious rites, while others have songs, incidents individually made by some people and for different reasons, and perhaps an Arab is no exception from the rest of the world, he was engaged in books of stories of this kind, he could introduce her to what is stated in the book of a curmudgeon sticking out let's go with us, dear readers, ask what he wrote about this.

Did not create a written translation of the Arab mention of cannibalism, the included scripts of the date and geography of the Arab that fell into the hands of our signals about the GM and the tribes of savages in the world remote from Earth in March this year, as well as the areas that occurred in the cities of Arab and foreign so that I have people to taste some kind of meat from the dead and dreams after I have spent all the food sources of others and maybe months, the story in this area is the story of Sinbad the sailor, where he and his fellow prisoners are, has a tribe the brutal says that he feeds delicious food to jerk off to the factor, but Sinbad refuses to eat, then he can escape later. Own (For more, see the Book of a Thousand Nights and Nights) And many researchers argue that Sinbad's stories are not purely fictional, but are inspired by true stories that were sold by Arab sailors who sailed the Indian Ocean to China and went through this long journey of dozens isolated islands and remote and inhabited tribes The savage hunted the heads of strangers who throw their unfortunate blood on these beaches and eat their flesh to gain more khaki strength and energy in accordance with their beliefs, and is confirmed and documented by researchers of European arrival this oh- so-in the sixteenth century. And, perhaps, one of the clearest and most ancient Arab sources about cannibalism is the book of the "vile" protruding (781-868 AD), which brings to us anecdotes about curmudgeons, their antics and ways of collecting money and folding and catching to spend at least a small part of them, and despite the fact that the book is competent to convey the stories of Scrooge and the curmudgeon, he gives us an overview and quickly for some eats meat, human sweat, and there are individual cases, of course, where they are remember it and disfigure it, as mentioned. Al-Jahiz in his book:

- And if a lion ate a dog, then what kind of meat do people have. And if you find a person from the tribe, then it comes out so ugly, so devoted that the whole tribe. They also praise everyone in the same way, although not the only one "

And giving us big-eyed examples of these incidents he says at the door of the food unsafe when:

- And the Curse of the Lion saved this amber, and eats the meat of people. The poet said in this:

When you eat, watch how the son of the server is the mouth and one after the circulation, out of the number five, four get nails like skin

Hasan told them:

If your secret is deceiving the exchange of not her mood, then please ask for a house to Haiyan people people who come into contact eat the side between their people and the dog and the Xian man

The poet has one radiance, and he wants to dress us with a lobe. And modern:

Wheel what a gift my attitude to work is the ostrich even ate childcare

And Er dress us with flabby boys, eating cornflower-blue flesh, the women shut up in the hostel from the front, said:

Hey my cousin, how do you know they don't make you count Sly eats the ribs I taste again I'm afraid of Bo when the blade is in the morning, Mr. Reid

Dress us the scarcity of eating women's meat. The dress of this Akram is the same when feeding a sly person with food, even if he is dying of hunger. And stories. The Hachima Taiyi families remaining at the time.

The poet said condemning a and such that:

Chastity eaten by his parents in line were his bones Cahill became the mother of his chastity

A hybrid of this lion of all, because of the sandbox of the FAAID girl, ibn Habib ibn Khalid bin lost, when he was eaten, her husband and her brother Abu Erb. They claimed that this was their path to anger and jealousy.

The daughter said the outline mourns him:

Avi to Roy did you want to think of pride, on the face of pride? Sandy was the wife of your team and the sister of the team, which is the infamous gold of ABBA Erb, how is the kinship between you and your brothers in the flesh of this scarcity?

He said::

The execution of a woman after the sandbox is a good son, the bubble comes to you safely and offers, then he became flesh from the gel in pots between you and alienation

Said Ibn Rabi's patent, 'brother is harmful to the photo of us, a quarter of the live connection is his brother. he said::

Oh, it refers to your house Rose's shop, oud is a cross, and if he called you to help remember the cutting edge of the underprivileged and now prays to the father of the people, then it's disgusting later with boyfriend

Abu men of this cousin.

He said in that famous Telson:

If the banks do not feed them at night, never eat human meat, he is free of good food, which interferes with the war drama

This door is often prepared. As we mentioned the proof of what we meant to him from the case classification. He also wanted to see him in the book populism, it is put there. "Over / mean P. 114

And so we see that Al-Jahiz can confidently incidents of cannibalism, when on the throne, and individual incidents were hated and reviled to such an extent that living and reviling the whole tribe, if one of the oldest members, on this heinous act, in contrast to some, and ... again he ate people's meat when normal, historians note, for example, that this is normal in China in the Middle Ages, and that human flesh, he knew that in the butcher's shops, the side of animal meat, just like historians, Spaniards about the routine of this year, when the tribes of the Caribbean Indians and which of them bought the term or the word "cannibalism - English means" meat-eating species ", and there is also a lot of news and texts related to incidents of this type and in different civilizations and eras, starting with a man, a Neanderthal, and you end an era, our present conditions call for our news Between the present moment and the last case of this type of crime.

Cheetah men .. lovers of human flesh

In ancient Egypt, the cheetah animal was revered, considering it one of the manifestations of the God of the "school of Ozzy", the judge of the dead, and, possibly, under the influence of this ancient doctrine, many African tribes adopted the leopard, a sacred animal that called the souls of the dead to peace and tranquility in the next world and in the 19th century a secret emerged that in some parts of Africa favored their personal cheetah. to recognize this community as terrible, which created fear and panic in much of the Black Continent for decades.

African society is a tribal society in which witchcraft has become of great importance, in most of the villages and cities of Africa, the sorcerer plays a major role in the life of these small groups, he is a doctor who expels evil spirits from the bodies of patients and is the defender of the village from evil creatures, many of whom gets into the head of an African simpleton man, and is a person who can speak in the fates of other people, he curses and conjures next to them or deciphers them, and in such a community they are superstitious and think their axioms, magic and supernatural power to think is a Muslim, everyone strives to get them, And one of the oldest myths known to some parts of our globe is that human flesh has a magical superhero and I am gutted, which means that he becomes strong and durable, and the male Panther range is the embodiment of that faith from which it begins to spread aggressively in parts of Africa such as Sie rra Leone, Nigeria and Liberia from the nineteenth century, of course, this does not mean that cannibalism was unknown in Africa before that date, since the excursions of the first space Africa in the seventeenth century, references were made in the books of European travelers from regions and some tribes usually there was eaten human flesh, However, this phenomenon did not know the prevailing dense and open distribution, and the organization of leopards also embodied in the community of people or people-Panthers (People-Leopards) Between 1900 - 1950 year of birth, and which illuminated the atmosphere of horror with hysteria in several African countries over a period of time, and killed hundreds of innocent people, and probably some of the emergence of this cult to the beliefs of magical and superstitious prevalent in the African society, others were of the opinion that this phenomenon is a reaction to the mystical colonialism and authority of the White Man. which has burdened Africans for centuries, since the advent of I were the slave ships that combed the shores of Africa for men and women and children and to cross the sea to keep them in slave markets in Europe and America.And this story of fear and inequality created in man a sense of African inferiority in front of a white man who seemed to him a miracle in everything, the cannons are deadly, and his ships with gigantic, shooting fire and flames, open fire burned thatched African huts and surrounded them with rubble, so the magic of the weather was the only way out for the African, who thought that it would kill his forces and make him an equal white man, and these rituals and beliefs were the main motivation for the behavior of the community of Panther people seeking supernatural power. , Cheetah Man not only wears the skin of a leopard and imitates his movements, but he believes that he is the reincarnation of the personality of the cheetah and she became a supernatural being, which does not hit with weapons and does not pierce his body with lead, and it was this belief that caused the fear of people and increased the number willing to join them.

One European researcher who studied this phenomenon in the twenties of the last century described the male Panther community and how they attacked their victims as follows:

- When you attack, the men of the community dress in leopard skins ... and sometimes they carry a net with them, drop it on the victim to provide it ... arm yourself with a knife, two iron sharp hands connecting them in the shape of cheetah claws, and carry a few short copies ... they usually attack at night and suddenly ... what they expect on the set when they attack is that it is almost impossible to drop the victim out of their hands ... soon they cut the victim's body, take out the meat and pass it on to the rest community members of men and women. "

It was an iron claw worn by men Panthers tearing the victim's body into an ugly one, even I, who sees, he thinks that the intruder is a real animal, and after collecting blood and flesh, the secrets in the depths of the jungle receded quickly and imperceptibly for Dance, where their rituals and rituals, magic and a joint meal of a person, accompanied by the drinking of blood, and for new participants who want to join the cult, drink a bottle of fresh human blood in the presence of others, in order to prove their merits in order to become leopard men, and since this process is associated with ritual magic, so that each member of the community had a leather bag called power (Borfima) Contain different things, they think that it has magical qualities, including a little egg white, a lack of blood and a person in addition to parts of the human body , penis blood and a few grains of rice, they believe this bag will bring the wearer wealth and power, physical hacks and long work, how much you can earn great respect from others and help in matters that the white man and his courts are engaged in, and in order not to lose the bag, the peculiarity of its magic had on the person. The cheetah is colored in human form and is stained with human blood from time to time.

Most of the physical testimonies and images of the sect's victims came from strange people who had lived in West Africa for so long, one of them was the German doctor Warner-Zhou, who worked as a doctor in remote areas of Liberia for three years over the past century and wrote a book about his experience, and also witnessed six cases of killing people by cheetahs and wrote about his participation in the body of one of the victims of the sect:

- There, on a mat inside the house, they found the body of a fifteen-year-old girl, her neck was torn with claws and teeth, her intestines were cut and the pelvic area was twisted, one had a leg and hip missing, the other did not leak out only a small part, but on the side of the victim's body there were parts of the tibial bone, the corpse looks like it was attacked by a predator, but a thorough examination did not fit this theory, I noticed, for example, that there is a small wound in the chest. the girl happened to sharpen the iron, since the lung was cut and removed from the inside of the body it is purely impossible for any animal. "

And with the rise of community crime and increased audacity, and used a law that peaked in the forties of the last century, devised governments to completely eliminate them, but they faced a big snag and people are afraid of the harsh people of the Panther, and despite temptation, I did not get any sensation or informed the community members, although they became famous and say that they openly confess their crimes in broad daylight, it was the population that thinks that the Panther Super people are right and that they will return to avenge them and their families, in the event of their death, a conflict with the police, and signed several incidents strengthened this belief among the people.In 1946, the police discovered the remains of thirteen human bodies near the house of one of the village heads, said that they were arresting him, and, fearing that it depended from the rest of the community, male cheetahs attacked his house and devoured his wife and daughter, and when the president's flag was damaged, they killed The young people suffered a heart attack and died of a stroke. But a big shift in the behavior of the population and you in relation to the sect occurred in 1947, when one of the nights one of the police officers who killed a member of the sect shot himself during an attack on his victim, and when people saw the body of a leopard man and already in full were convinced that the members of the community were ordinary people and did not possess any superpowers, so witnesses quickly began to filter through police stations and aspiring community members fell one by one, and with the decisions of the 1950s, the name of the panther guys turned into a memory of the page with the inscription "Panther". the horror of a story curled up forever.

In Papua New Guinea ... Grieving for the dead includes cutting them up and eating their meat !!

Imagine, dear reader, that you are invited to the funeral of one of the deceased, and while the time of serving lunch or dinner on the spirit of the deceased takes his family and friends out of the coffin, and then cuts him and attracts the public to devour his flesh, and they abundantly shed tears in his memory !! Do not study and do not laugh, this is not a joke and not a fictional horror story, but usually real practiced for centuries by members directly in Papua New Guinea and was the key reason to avoid a strange disease, and the killer among them made a significant contribution to gradually eradicating this tribe is the custom of eating human flesh.

Papua New Guinea (Papua New Guinea) - This is a state that occupies the eastern part of the island of New Guinea, located in the Pacific Ocean north of mainland Australia, which is the second largest island in the world, and has the difference of this state with hundreds of primitive tribes, living in the jungle and jungle in the rain thickly isolated from the world for millennia, as well as the difference of each tribe, language and habits of their own, numbering more than 850 different languages in this small piece of land. And as a result of the isolation of these tribes from the outside world, their primitive way of life, based on collecting wild fruits and hunting for animals, remained, and each tribe was under a conservative sphere of influence and often there were wars and intertribal feuds that controlled this influence.

Known to sailors and traders in the South Asian region of Papua New Guinea since ancient times, and they often went to catch a beautiful bird and a unique bird of paradise (Bird of Paradise), but these sailors did not dare to go beyond the coastal areas because of their fear of the tribes of the beast living in the forests, where they eat people, there are many horror stories about the love of the inhabitants of the forest for savages, they eat human flesh and know the human head as a decoration in the house. And in the seventeenth century Europeans came to the island and colonized the coastal regions until the nineteenth centuries, when they began some excursions and missions available in the forest, it was a journey inside the jungle, dangerous, and often it was white people attacked the tribes brutality that did not stop killing and devouring some of them, But despite the risks, the mission succeeded in drawing the world's attention to life in this secluded place, which has helped scientists in various fields to study the laws of life and tradition nations and customs of the primitive tribes who inhabited it, and took on board a living example of what human life was like in antiquity, and of the most important manifestations of primitive life that attracted the attention of scientists and researchers, is the phenomenon of cannibalism, practiced by most tribes in the forests of Papua New Guinea ... (The scientists' front interest, in particular, was that the tribe remained isolated from the world in the bush until the 1950s and was their exercise of a ritual, a light unique one involving the eating of human flesh with the mouth, which uttered the face of the tribe members with their breath while it did not meet with the women of his relatives around him, and they separated his arms, legs and head from his body, and then they fried several steaks and ate them, and also ate the heart, liver and internal organs, since the decoder has no special place, it is the most delicious part of eating the mouth to avoid the spiritual body of a person.dead until women tell them to break the skull and pull it out as soon as possible, every intention is still hot and fresh, and women usually tear off the body parts of their children, and sometimes flee, Of course, at the feast the tribe also includes prisoners of war from other tribes, but they mostly rely on the dead bodies of members of the same clan and are mainly limited to women and children, so as the body of the dead should be the sound of disease, they do not seek the flesh of people who die due to disease and fear of infection.

The cost that members of primitive tribes did when they knew that humans and exploration missions at home did not eat human flesh was to devour human flesh for something inherent in them and they responded to the advice to give up this habit, saying that they find no reason why there is human flesh for them, like other meat is tastier than meat, The taste of his mission resembles that of sweet potatoes, and the other resembles the taste of pork chops, as it has on the rest of the meat in the ease of digestibility and deliciousness on it where his fellow tribesmen are involved say that devouring large amounts of animal meat can feel that the person will be sick, and sometimes in the urge to puke like human flesh, you can eat whatever you want from him until his stomach is full and you have to swallow more and you won't feel bad.

Despite the addiction to the women of the tribe, who are accustomed to devouring human flesh, however, the tribe had to leave this year due to an outbreak of a fatal disease among its members, who called this designation Korea (Kuru) And its meaning is trembling or shaking, because the disease causes a level jump in the patient's body with pain in the head and bones and joints and a situation requiring over time the patient becomes incapable of movement and swallowing, and even breathing and ends with death after almost a year of the appearance of the first symptoms of the disease. At first I thought at that moment that the disease is the curse of evil spirits and is not associated with the world of cannibalism, so they continue to devour the bodies of their dead and the number of patients continues to increase, prompting doctors and researchers to interest in studying the disease and reaching it occurs due to an imbalance in a specific gene, a change in the work of proteins in the brain is searched for and affects its functionality in a similar way to what happens in the body Mad cow disease and reassured doctors that eating human flesh is considered a major contributor to the outbreak and spread of the disease, and evidence of this is that women make up about ninety percent of the total number of injuries, and this is because the tribe usually devouring human flesh has immediate costs to be limited to women.

Promoted the fear of disease, besides the arrival of civilization and civilization in these remote regions, the left usually eat human flesh and it gradually disappeared and as a result, the number of designers who are in Korean has decreased, with the exception of a few cases that appeared in the nineties, and also in 2004 and seen by some as evidence that some of the instant they still exercise normally ate human flesh is a secret, but there is no concrete evidence to support this claim.

Self-cannibalism ... Can a person eat himself ?!

Then I put my hand to my mouth and began to eat myself. "

This was the novel's final proposal (committee) for the creation of the God of Abraham. The committee ruled on the hero of history who eats himself, because of his excess of ambition, which exceeded his potential, expanded his geek beyond the battle and in spite of the committee. This tragic ending is not very bizarre, and not all that simple. in fact, there are many cases when it happens to eat a person or the animal itself, or, more precisely, parts of its body, and this is what we will consider in these lines.

Have you ever wondered, dear reader, how good his hand is when fried with tomato sauce? Have you ever imagined that one day you would eat a piece of his right thigh with spices and mayonnaise? !! ... The answer would be no, of course, because such disciplines do not believe only in Homo sapiens, but as much as her abnormality and conversation with her at breakfast, however there are many documented cases for her and will be analyzed in this article ...

Ask to eat the object so that parts of its body stop being themselves. Self-cannibalism. Cancer must eat an object that is of the same sex. As in the case of tribes of cannibals, as it happens when animals eat the bodies of their dead, belonging to the same species.

We begin the animal world, where the animal relies on knowledge or crickets eat their wings like a mouse eats its tail in case of severe hunger. And the octopus animal sometimes with a bacterial or viral infection makes him feel intense itching in his hands, so he eats to get rid of them. But in the case of the octopus, it's easy to grow arms back after that. Sharks also have something like that, if it crawled out of their blood, it goes crazy if the smell of blood is such that the shark is trying to eat itself along with their colleagues from sharks, which they will take care of you, will devour it! Peter Banksy's description of this scene is described in detail in his novel "Jaws" .... And also the Snake The Rat The Rat Snake An attempt to devour itself in North America, if it happened in families and that through the dovetail continue to devour itself so that it can swallow two-thirds of your body and then die. !!

In addition to pathological cases, we ordinary people have a kind of cancer of the self when we bite our nails, or when we snap our lips, or we boulders with our teeth to the crust, or when we eat the appendages of the skin, when our nails. And the human body itself always speaks to swallow dead cells from the tongue and cheek, which is also a kind of cancer of itself.

There have been cases of illnesses that lead police officers to devour parts of his body, such as "feel-Harn" syndrome, which is a rare genetic disorder that causes the source to bite his lips, tongue and fidget with fingernail movements. Some people are also known to eat hair on their heads , and this is called Rapunzel syndrome, by the way, Rapunzel is the hero of one of the stories of the Brothers Grimm, who was locked in a high tower and her lover got her hair from the tower to the counter!

There are healthy people indulging in cancerous self-will, as are some anomalous groups of vampire nerds. the fact that they drink blood in a ritual of exotic beauty, and in some primitive societies mothers eat the placenta after giving birth, there are many people who drink urine of their own, which are members of the Thunderer in the armies who carry out this command in situations of war and family and getting lost in desert and keeps them alive. And there is the case of the famous eccentric named "Bernd Brands" all his will, another German loves to eat human flesh in order to tear it to pieces and eat it, and he is alive and even share in eating flesh, but rather so that "BARS" at the request of his killer, to cut off his penis, the executive through the bite of his teeth, and then several and present him and savor his taste !! And there is another reality - not without wit it is possible to include oneself in the box of cancer, and there is at that time the intention of the cello artist "Marco Nearest" with a group of friends for dinner at his house, but the food was kind of strange and represented a popular sauce from coils of fat ... this fat was a human deficiency, it is unlikely that the artist himself could have disposed of it somewhere in the process of liposuction, carried out several months ago, but he kept the company in the demilitarized zone to eat it.

There are also those who had Cancer themselves against their will, as part of torture, or during captivity in war. In 1991, Sudan makes some young people have ears, where a swarm of victims of ethnic cleansing in southern Sudan, that part of the militia was to keep young people and children, and cut off their ears and force them to chew and swallow, but because they do not "hear the word of the copyright holders and do not listen to the orders of the police," says that immigrants from Europe to America in the seventeenth century they forced Indians prisoners to eat their genitals, and in the Europe of the Middle Ages there is a character named "Elizabeth Bathory Erzhebet Bathory - She lived in the sixteenth century and forced her workers to eat their flesh when they lured the little peasant into her big castle and then locked the doors and took them to the torture room, Roy that she made them bite and bite their hands and feet so that they forget to cook meat from bones and fall to the ground, and then they ate these parts and licked the ground. In the movie "Hannibal Anthony Hopkins" we saw Dr. Hannibal Lecter, and he says that he roasts parts of the brain his victim and cooks them with a spoon, in one of the most gruesome scenes in film history!

A deadly journey ... a convoy of travelers' meat!

Hunger is disbelief! ... This proverb sometimes hits the justification for the actions of the hungry, which involves any work to fill your stomach with food, even if it is what you eat, is reviled by others, even from different religions they sell their adherents to eat information, if it saved their souls from destruction, and one of the information that must be agreed upon by all religions, laws and morals is human flesh, but people have replaced it since then, when in the areas of disasters and immunities of war, especially when there is nothing to eat the Swan, and its story today is about the column of unfortunates surrounded by snow in the mountains no longer exists. In front of the passenger, who was only devouring the meat of his colleagues, the story of the terrible journey brought his passengers closer together about which of them should be stabbed and eaten !!.

For centuries, the ships of Europe were dense in large numbers of migrants home, sailing across the Atlantic to provide protection to humanity on the east coast of the United States, they were aliens, people of different stripes and nationalities, exhausted by wars and revolutions on the Old Continent, so we, their faces are turned to the New World in search of a better life, and years after years the congregations of millions of these European seers on the east coast of the United States have even enlarged their cities and crowded their roads, overwhelmed unemployment and spread poverty, and diminished business and wealth opportunities. While those cities and States in the east are adding to their population day after day, it is the western parts of the United States that unleashed a new reel (1) stepping into a human closed country, which is why I took convoys of migrants fleeing the rush of the race to get before her, and it was a false advertisement, and not just a memorial and celebration of the role of outstanding and effective in pushing and motivating many pastors and gullibles for this mass migration after this picture of those distant lands is arid as the soil is rich in precious metals and a masterpiece gold case. The mines that produce alien shovels and chisels to carry their wealth over their heads to the density of illusion.

On May 8, 1846, he left the American town of Springfield with a small column of nine wooden carts drawn by cows, a distribution and about 33 male, child and female traveling among themselves, the entire families of the inferiority farm of George six and five and his brother Jacob, and also their neighbor businessman James Reed. If these people decided to move with their families and everything they had to migrate the long and arduous 2500 miles around California in the Far American West, and they planned to achieve goals that in only four months, to start the journey just after the spring rains stop and ends before winter. Time was an important factor in the success of their journey, because any delay meant that winter was about to push them and try their snow centers in the valleys and distant mountains. They knew that there are many rivers and life in the arid and Rocky mountains, that it must be traded safely, there is also the risk of bandits translating caravans for plunder and looting, as well as attacks by disgruntled

Indians due to the capture of white settlers on their lands. But good and encouraging for George Donner and his comrades was their perception that they were not alone on their long journey, that caravans of migrants flow like a ladder of shame, carrying with them thousands of people from different parts of the country to a common goal, and before a long escort inferiority small, which melted in the stream, flowing non-stop and under the banner of the largest caravan, led by a man named William Russell.

Russell's convoy worked for two months along the California railroad line, until it reached the Little Sandy River, where the timing is harsh, when George and his comrades are taken there for several days, misreading them and tragically separating from Russell's convoy and the big and having gone alone through the old Hastings skating pillars, thinking that they would choose the remaining distance of their journey from them, they joined in their adventures with the indiscretion that some passengers of another convoy, bringing number 87, travel by distribution on 23 carts, get settled in a new caravan led by George Donner.
On August 31, 1846, the convoy, New through the old one, was Christian for the first week, hungry and encouraging, but the trouble did not take long to be recognized while crossing the desert, Great Salt and the surrounding mountains to find several cows and horses and caused significant damage to a number vehicles, and the convoy was attacked by Indians, Saint one of the passengers breathing his across the road, and did not reach the caravan to Nevada only painstakingly late three weeks from the scheduled date providing the nerves of the people, and they share the blame and the jumper. And they killed one of the passengers on the arm of James Reed after a violent quarrel broke out between them at Mr. Reed in his caravan and his departure from the family.

In late October, they reached the trail leading to the Sierra Nevada mountain range along the California border, George Donner and his companions knew they had reached this point of their journey too

late, so they walked at full speed, hoping to meet the
towering mountains before than to study their winter, but luck let
them down this time, because that day only one of the leaders
from the highlands took abundant snow.

I was well aware that their journey had now turned into a frantic
race with death, so I urged the travelers to continue their journey,
but when in the evening they got tired and exhausted from the
meeting, women were looking for women, tired of the inferiority of
that camp by the lake, now known as the lake of inferiority - they
hoped break the ice at night, so the guy seemed to be reluctant, but
he himself expected the worst, and established in his intuition,
because it snowed all night. And when in the morning there was a
huge mass of ice, reaching a height of twenty feet, the stomach
could be filled.
Trapped and the convoy went down completely, covered the snow
in both directions that can usually progress and return, and certifies
passengers that they will spend their winters in this remote
location and secluded from Earth, and realized that the amount of
revenue is possible after I took a ration of convoy food, mastered
gradually, until I completely sold including men to slaughter the
animals of the caravan of cows and horses, until they all came in a
short period, and until there is no more food, try some of the men
to hunt wild animals but that took him from squirrels and small
birds, so as not to miss the hunger of more than eighty people, half
of them women and children. In the end, they had to lock
themselves in a caravan to devour the bark of trees and branches,
and some boiled the skins of dead animals and ate its stew.

In the midst of the despair that hit the caravan, some of the
passengers decided to take the marathon route to get help and
bring rescue teams. The task was difficult because the
nearest settlement was a fraction of a mountain 160 miles away,
and that distance from the Rocky Mountains and cold snow caps
without adequate food is synonymous with impossibility in the

eyes of many. But ten men - eight whites and two Red Indians - and the five women accompanying them share the success they have chosen to continue on their journey, whatever the results. They understand that the chances of their arrival at the goal and success from hunger and cold look very small, so they chose a name for themselves that indicates the difficulty of their task and is "hope for the unfortunate", and set off on their journey, which, having some food and some old guns and shoes for walking in the snow, they made themselves from the bones and skins of dead animals.

The delightful members of "hope for the unfortunate" nine days in the snow before they realize they are walking on a treadmill and are completely lost in the middle of this white carpet of Infinity that surrounds them on all sides, much of the food has been spent since then how three days choose hunger, stop their intestines and pressure, and exhaustion, and Rahu are in a speech that the distance between the shoulders on his face tells to do and rests on the tree trunk resists falls, in Java they are threatened from all sides and hump , will those unfortunate people think about doing it? a way to survive, and they came to solve quirks, the closest thing to the dream that we hear about in myths and legends, When it suddenly gets dark on that evening when these passengers fly, hungry and exhausted, around the fire that they kindled in the open, and they agreed to cut straw between them (2), and the loser must curb the appetite and be eaten by the winners !. And it was Patrick Dolan, 35 years old, this bad luck that pulls the straw of the loser in the rally for that death, and you, dear reader, can imagine the horror that the poor fellow saw in his demanding heart, and in the eyes of his comrades, threats like wolves preparing to gnaw at the flesh of their prey. What happened after that, perhaps you do not know that only Allah, the value of the group "Hope for the Unfortunate" they said later that none of them came to their hearts to kill Mister Dolan, and he did not touch him, it hurts that night, but the horror and obsession that infected the man and his fear of colleagues prompted him to run away and hide alone in the forest, and the next morning they found a group on his frozen body curled up in a ball when the trunk of one of the trees early her with a knife cut and skinned, and then they "party" grill finely eat part of the pulp of the body and save the rest for the coming days.

Of course, there are many doubts overshadowing the death or murder of Mr. Dolan, most people believe that the story of his escape and his death, renewed in the forest, is a different story of his colleagues, who most likely committed suicide that night, but later denied this because of the heinous nature of the crime and the fear of being tried and executed by hanging for murder.

But the journey of death and horror does not end there, on the day when the murdered Mr. Dolan abandoned India, the two accompanying the group eat his flesh, and the phenomenon that all mankind has caused disgust and fear in two men after another, and the balance between the trees of the forest ... Then nine days were spent, during which Mr. Dolan's flesh got hungry and exhausted by the Hope for the Unfortunate members again, while watching the loss, but just as serious, you must make more human flesh! While one of the ladies of the group was walking alone between the trees in the forest, probably to pee, I suddenly discovered that India is Iran that fled last week and they stop their breath between the snow, and the alleged survivors of the group. that India was needed because of hunger and cold and they didn't have to live more than two hours, so they put two bullets in each of them's heads, perhaps out of kindness and compassion !! Then their cut bodies are piled on the wheel, and soon the fragrant atmosphere of the distant jungle smells of barbecue again.

Like the story of Mr Dolan's death, the story of the flight to India, two are in the woods and find what they need after nine days, they seem very naive and do not affect anyone, and it is most likely that these two men were killed and devoured them because they were more the weak point among the members of the group "this is a scoundrel", the Red Indians at that time had no rights and that the white man was tried for the murder of the Red Indian.

On January 18, about a month after its launch, the "Hope of the Unfortunate" finally reached one of the settlements, only seven survived, and the funny thing is that out of ten men who went with the group at the very beginning, only two survived. as well as five women, so why none of them, and of course what women had to clean up lol, they ate the meat of the poor !! And the survivors are fighting after they ate the meat of their colleagues of the dead need to stay alive, but they denied that they killed any of them, claiming that eight people (one of them a boy in the twelfth) all died of cold, hunger and disease.

After the arrival of the "this scoundrel" group, there are four rules of rescue in relation to an inferior convoy besieged in the mountains, not rescue operations, easy due to the primitive means used at the time and the crossed area and the seriousness of its situation. During the first meal, the rescuers were shocked by what they saw within the camp, they survived, trapped like the ghosts of the dead, their faces turned pale, and their eyes sunken, their bodies turned into skeletons, it was impossible to distinguish them from the bodies of the dead, only their breath became restless.

In and around the carriages of the caravan, the bodies of people and animals were scattered, some human bodies were mutilated and dislocated by the hips and thighs, it was clearly visible that the survivors had to eat the meat of the dead.
The number of survivors was 47 people, including the wife of James Reed and his five children, since the deaths were 39, including George himself, inferior, who died due to the rotting operation that fell into his hand, and therefore his wife may have been eaten by someone named Louis Cyber, and Louis this last person left the camp with a rescue convoy fourth and after surviving a threat from several people, because he had to eat from the bodies of his loved ones and relatives in the camp.

Today, next to the lake of inferiority, there is a monument created in memory of those displaced persons who died in the death camp. It is true that their story is accompanied by many atrocities, and it is also true that the journey of those men and women who embarked on a painful journey through the snow to get help was accompanied by many heinous incidents, but you must remember in the end that these atrocities were committed out of necessity and that these simple people, they were not lovers of human flesh, and I do not imagine this once, but, as mentioned earlier at the beginning of the article, hunger is unbelief, and life is dear to the hearts of most people. resist the temptation to curse some people have it in eternal comfort and confidence that these blasphemers see them clinging to them until their last breath and done without dear and precious in times of disaster - And maybe, if you know us, we too are to the same circumstances, which they took, got into an inferiority convoy, but having something to eat ... and we were able to cook and fry ... you to the belly line ... maybe .. who knows ?!

1.Many states to the West and South of what is now the United States of America (over a third of those currently surveyed) are in fact land occupied by America from Mexico during the American-Mexico War (1846-1848), that war , which was lost by Mexico in its half of the territory (Texas - New Mexico - Colorado - Arizona - Utah - Nevada - California).

2 - a bunch of straws, or wild grass, is taken and cut to different lengths, and then travels between their heads and includes the palm of one of the people, so that he cannot make voters know or guess the length, and the loser is the one who pulls out the least amount of peel ...

Do any of you like to eat your dead brother's flesh?

Eating human flesh ..
What a terrible time ... bring up all the problems of nausea in self-healing .. That's ok .. But it causes some other souls to see that pleasure remains .. Yes, someone eats human flesh, but savor it. We know this happens in primitive societies. now..as among the tribes (Zulu) and some primitive tribes in Bush, Africa and in Latin .. Already the lining allowed scientists to designate this (cannibalism) and translate (eating the flesh of the same sex), which comes from the Spanish word Caribbean, describing the tribes (Caribbean) of the Indians spoken of by the seafarers (Christopher Columbus). The Moors have eaten human flesh throughout history, in several places and situations, such as:

1. during events 2. in the Civil War 3. some primitive tribes 4 - as a kind of exaggeration in harming the enemy .. where he eats from the flesh of the defeated 5 - the belief of some that those who eat the flesh of enemies transfer their abilities to them (cross) 6 - like the weather religious or funeral rituals 7 - like the behavior of my sexual

Here are some historical examples:

1-found: human bones in vessels for cooking the old half a million a year in China .. Among the most famous tribes known for this activity historically the tribe (Anasazi.) In North America 2-it is said that (James Cook), who was killed by the inhabitants (Hawaii), was eaten 3 - You can eat human flesh a kind of reverence for the dead, as some tribes in (New Zealand) do, they glorify the memory of the dead who eat the brains..after that person dies, do not post such meetings around your body and do not sing some religious hymns, and then removed the witch like a dead brain and equally among the mourners to eat them. 4. (Raoul de Kahn) historian of the crusade: (It was our people in Al-Maarr who cook adult Muslims in pans .. and the boys in Said Wells roasted two) And the Muslim population (al-Numan) in (Syria) ..

....

In the modern era:

I missed the many serial killers of cannibalism like:
1 - (Armen) The art of a computer German, who confessed to killing and eating a person in early 2001, where she met her until announced on internet sites, is that he asks a young strong man between the eighteenth and thirtieth to eat .. He then told (Mavis) that after that he killed his sympathy for him, but that did not calm the affair of disgust that struck the German people .. The wonderful Iyad of my brother of benevolence mentions this fact in detail in a large article .. 2 - (Albert Fish), who raped and killed and ate many children in his twenties, and he said he felt pleasure from sex and massive as a result. 3-Russian mobster (Andrei Chikatilo) who killed 53 people at least between 1978 and 1990 4 - like the famous case of Japan (Issi Sagawa), who killed a Danish Sorbonne student (Rene dried) and then ate him, and his doctors got off crazy .. and therefore cannot be prosecuted .. she was returned to (Japan) where she was in a mental hospital for ten months, I went out after

and even today on the big mission wells that it was his father's intervention, being a man of influence in Japan .. 5. during World War II, many cases of cannibalism were recorded and documented .. for example:

1 - City (Leningrad) lecture for 872 days between 194 2 .in at first, people and soldiers ate birds, rats and pets, and after its entry into force, people resorted to cannibalism, which prompted the city police to create a unit to combat cannibalism. 2. in February 1943, almost one hundred thousand German soldiers were taken out as prisoners of war in the USSR (Siberia) .. There was the area of the Soviets, the Germans did not even keep them only five thousand .. Even those who survived after eating, survived because that the Soviets came and devoured them as a result of a disease that later became extinct in their belief in this ... 3.During World War II, stories were documented of how some people found sausage on human nails that talked about the use of human meat in their manufacture ..

4 - Many testimonies and reports were documented that were made after World War II during investigations and trials that were about war crimes. It was reported that Japanese soldiers would have to eat the meat of captured Allies during the war in many regions of East Asia. according to the historian (Yuko Tanaka): (Eating human flesh was systematically carried out by whole detachments of soldiers under the command of officers) 5 - sometimes the meat was cut into human biology .. Here is a notarized affidavit made by the guest (Lance Nike): You are part of the allied forces and captured by the Japanese in (New Guinea) .. The Japanese started taking prisoners, every day they kill and eat one of us .. I ate about 100 certified for the duration of our families, and then they moved the door to the new norm 50 miles away, and recover from the 10 accredited from the disease .. Then usually the Japanese choose the prisoners and the fields, and they transport the selected individuals to a separate cottage, where pieces of their flesh are separated from their bodies while they were alive - and

then they are thrown into a deep hole among their hideous screams and they come down and they are cooked in front of them and eaten until he dies later

6-The last documented case that occurred during World War II was recorded in February 1945 when he forced 30 Japanese soldiers on an island (leaf) Japanese to marry their Major (Matoba) and General (than) Admiral (Mori) and (Yoshi) and (Terra emulator) to kill and eat five members of the slack and an American .. This reality was different ... which surpassed the design in its ugliness, where they would cut out parts of the liver or the smile of the sides to only keep five alive for a few days to ensure you get fresh meat .. He was convicted on Friday during an investigation they had in 1947, and they were tried by a war crimes tribunal in Sana'a! ... But what about being alone? It is said in his holy book: (O YOU who believed, avoid most of the shadow of sin, did not spy, and there are some of the few who eat the flesh of their brother who died here, and God, if God is faithful) Al-Hujurat ... verse (12)

The whole key to that verse that replaces the parent site of the base image .. I mean explained .. looting, full of gossip and gossip, you ate the flesh of the raped dead. So it was said: (here) .. Without going into the details of the religious field, here we say that not a single commentator mentioned that one of the people actually eats the dead .. But the whole dog on it is just a fictional image .. No one searched for this word (here) .. Falkor does not mean abstinence .. Refrain from slander and gossip .. Also refrain from eating the flesh of the dead .. Despite the explicit prohibition on eating the dead in verse: (Only you are forbidden to be dead meat and blood and pork and the fact that people are not-God, this is not Bagh and usually there is no sin on you, if God is Forgiving, Merciful) Al-Bakara ... verse (173) Allah also said: (Forbidden you are dead, blood , and pork, and the fact that besides Allah, as well as installation and eat only seven clever you and the massacre of the monument and the SSC-Koran, that fornication of the day those who did not believe in religion despair do not be afraid OSCE today I have completed my religion for you, I finished the race my favor and approved for you as a religion of Islam, it is forced into a non-human, because God is forgiving, merciful) Surah ... verse (3) However, the turbulence here is consistent with the word (here) in the first verse .. Anyone whom God has authorized to eat the flesh of the dead in order to preserve their life and not die of hunger .. First, what we see in our minds when we mention this is Jeff's dead animals like deer and rabbits .. Or even cats and dogs ... but has this already happened ?? You made Muslims eat dead people. And when did it happen ?? I Have there been such areas in the Islamic world as before? .. This is what you will do now .. Just keep reading.

A researcher of Islamic history discovers that historians have changed fashion a lot .. And many of their valor, the researcher notes, is that the history of the territories that entered the Islamic world actually began not only from the end of the second century AH, this is normal .. Because historians were busy with the prophetic biography and biography of the companions of the correctly ruled caliphs and the result of the Islamic conquests at that time ... and then the founding of the Umayyad dynasty and its successors, and then the Abbasid state .. However, the survival of the Abbasid caliphs for a long period of time allowed historians to devote yourself to the events of other significant disasters .. For example, drought or scarce any holding rains can lead to areas ... and floods and snowfalls, earthquakes, storms, lightning strikes and raids of locusts and pests, epidemics, fires, etc. But this did not prevent historians from the gold reserve for some and the plague in Islam, like: 1 - the siege of the apostle and the division of dad's disciple for 3 parts years..so he told historians: (Until he got to people, making incredible efforts, and even they heard their boys begging behind people, and they ate foliage and an active stone on their bellies) 2 - lean, which happened in the city in the previous year of the attack, so that people bought it to the Prophet, peace be upon him, conveyed him a prayer for rain 3-in the ashes of the city in the year he (639 peace) and prayed for him the prince of the believers (Umar ibn Khattab) about the prayer for rain and wrote by the time to do this ... and continued to lean menacingly for 9 months so historians wrote: (So people were calculated as breathing over the first site even that he ate the skin of a dead fried ... his tumor of bone powder was Ison) 4. plague (points) on the network in the same year mentions some other plagues that occurred in Iraq and away from the stream and Mecca in He (699 world) .. And the truth is, we got this clearly from the writings of his son Isaac , the expected year (he) (768), the load of the middle year (he) (823), Hisham's son (o n) (828); and Ibn Sa'd of the expected year (he) (845 m) and his middle year (he) (855 world) and the third year (he) (889) and the cashew of the expected year (he) (892 world) and Abu Hanifa line in (he) (895) then .. Show history textbooks, especially famous books (yearbooks) of the original source about the places of natural disasters and accidents during the Middle Ages Islamic beginning of the book (History of paintings and kings) Tabari and ends (flowers through the events of centuries) by son Las projected years (year he) (1522), t. So, people, companions of the Messenger of Allah, ate carrion. mice..so in many ways that's why they dug, looking for her .. It all depends on the ugliness of his acceptable .. But does it come to the cannibalism of the dead? Yes, unfortunately .. This is exactly what happened in many areas that have struck the Islamic world throughout history .. I eat people a little, a little .. And the law that governs man is the law of the jungle .. Where the strong eats, the weak is not really released .. And not only that, but also what you will see in a few minutes. But the worst thing that happened in the cities and regions was that the nursery was radiating them to the consequences of (Europe) dark at that time. To (Iraq), and (Egypt), and (Algeria), and (Al-Andalus) .. Do not be surprised, I believed and said: (Hunger is wrong) There is such a famous saying: (H bellies await brains and an hour of fate, blind sight) When you are about to die of hunger ... trust that you will not stop your mind from doing nothing to prevent your death ... even if you are .. Will you dress the nursery and dedicate yourself to what religions and divine laws gave us .. Show your image to naked Real .. Just a predator ... a monster crusher is not only about staying alive in the middle of the jungle in which we live .. And who said :(The flood in Halle put my son under your feet) .. Said the poet AMI cynical (die my lover and obsessed with discussion) no, don't catch the flu And .. So, how these words were honest in the soul of all ancestors .. Do not be surprised .. ... this is a real person .. People of the Stone Age .. - Quite right ... Now let's turn to the dark side of the history of our ancestors, as I said .. This o will be on the hinges .. Because the polisher was too much to count or count .. But I'll try to be brief .. You won't remember everything ... folders .. it's just that .. I see that everything this is equally important .. I ... repeat .. do not understand ... maybe the fact is stranger than any fiction .. The question remains open: If we were in their place, I would live in the same circumstances, would we recognize them? ... I leave the answer to you .. Before I begin, I would like to point out that my brother's wonderful Iyad can eat about cannibalism aside and the calibration of tribes to each other of this heinous act, As mentioned by Al-Jahiz in his books ..

Now let's start from the East. Where do you guys know the beauty of the East from .. Let's go to (Iraq) .. Come to Mesopotamia .. Let's go to (Baghdad) and (Basra) .. But this is not (Baghdad) civilization .. (Baghdad) witch .. This (Baghdad) is different .. (Baghdad) is different. Completely different...

Before we begin to review the disasters of these areas, let me tell you about some of the disasters that have hit the special (Baghdad) and general (Iraq) areas .. Of course, I will not mention all natural disasters .. But as I said, I will mention only the most important ..

Mention of Jamal al-Din Abu group, Abdul Rahman ibn Muhammad ibn al-Jawzi in (he) (1201) in the table (enter the History of Kings and Peoples), there are many who want epidemics that befell the people (Iraq) .. For example, it says:

1 - earthquakes: Signed in Baghdad in He (1153), the horrific earthquake left more than two hundred and thirty thousand dead, even usually on their own business, so that their graves are crying

because ... people thought it shook the coast .. 2 - flooding of rivers and the coast: A - the stream is red (Baghdad) and in a year it (849) is free for everything and for nothing even pours into the Tigris River, changing the color of the Tigris water to zero and this lasted three days and frightened people so that water it for a long time .. B - and the flood - the greatest in the history of the Tigris happened in its year (1174) and was the most serious flood experienced (Baghdad) in antiquity, since the NSP of water in the Tigris is about 23 cubits, it was the highest value recorded by the duration of the flood of more than five weeks, and remained with it throughout the month of Ramadan and the first week of the month of Shawwal, and during this the Tigris and Euphrates and the water of Baghdad, East and West, and for the rainy and cold so it was said what some some of the trustworthy weights were seven pounds .. Many people died and livestock drowned and died from transplantation and the role of water, buildings, waste, many of them even reached two thousand gifts of erosion in their role, other people threatened the role if there is a fear of it destruction is more than rain demolition..the house is located on its inhabitants Fahey your dog straight from the palace of the caliphate, the mosque, but the damage is also done in the cemetery so it was said: (And look at graves like him, there is a heart of the collection, we have the money there are as great as the orthopedic care of tombstones) Filled with layers of water for people to worship the boat, take refuge in the deserts, and the high hills are considered Oman and high prices. 3 - tilting and turning off the rain: Lin, most of which also fell into the Tiger, throughout its history, and it was in that year (1177) and even went out to the islands of the fate in which the era of people like us was :(The ship was washed ashore in the middle of the Tigris has the right to leave) So the rain came, in the winter of the year, just like in the spring without Qatar, but this is not a singing thing, and the click of a year-long bridge and the thinning of the implant poured rain on it, increased the price bread, barley and praised by many people who came out to see the creation of many reactionary people who came from (connector) to the rear to sell them, they increased their prices. 4 - severe storms: Free came, tense in the second half of Ramadan in He (mid-March in 1177 of the world) In what era did we stay for a week, and then gusts of wind followed, shook the world with great force, then bought the ascended earth so that heaven would give Pisces first yellowish and the wind became famous for long hours ... then collaborated and an angry red color appeared in the sky derivative from the time of dawn to get to the Sun, and then it was shown in the absence of the Moroccan sun, this is kind of healing, but it is most of all in red we did not see how you, how the blood and escalation seems to be illuminated under the cloud, then you will find its places, like the light of the sun and the duration remained ... The shown columns look like people on the outskirts of the sky as if it rises from the earth wasting human suffering And they thought, that it is the wind that drives people to the lawn mower .. The night of the thirtieth came, because she is and could not see the crescent moon of some people of the month according to desires and the Crescent, plus abbreviated The feeling in Bolshoi and Van of the people who raised him. Signed many roles and died with a whole group of people..so there is a fear that there will be a resurrection..lasted a month..then it was cool and rain poured from the sky all day, and then Angela) 5 - fires: Big fires that engulfed Baghdad, and most of these were dense until they reached 14 fires during the seven years of the seventh century AH between the years 500 and 570 of the attack, which is a significant number considering that (Baghdad) was the capital of the Islamic Caliphate at the time ..

Over the words of Ibn al-Jawzi .. And all this is about the fact that the cause of decay and ruin is strangled by thousands of people and subjects, even people thought that these were some signs of the times, except that this does not concern us here. What does it mean in our this and our that focus on hunger and what it can do to a person .. So let's now explore the history of those areas in which Baghdad was born throughout its history, Islamic .. Lost find out what you can do with hunger , a human being .. So how does a man starve ... Before showing this to you, I want to say that even those domain scourging was really the most prolific, so I will only mention a few of them .. For example: 1-according to Ibn al-Jawzi in the table (alter in the history of the Kings and nations), which reads the following :: About the lesions caused by locusts, and talked about it .. We mention, for example :: (Meeting (Basra) in He (854), swarms of locusts exterminated the implant from people in his request for the night couples rain and a storm of wind 1300 of them died between a man and a woman and a boy .. That year he (923) in the locust rear around (Iraq) and his numerous corrupted Gala .. And the people went out in their request to eat th .. Then he met the black locust (Baghdad) in 331 (942) and was during the famine and epidemic of Baghdad, and found in it the poor help of the people with the intensity of the high cost of bread .. In the summer of the same year he (955) to the back of Grady many aspects (Baghdad) came to the summer water harvests affected trees and fruits .. and the poor eat .. And the locust pandemic in the spring of the first year he (955), the people of drought and the increase in value, and the discovery of locust that he grew vegetables and bought it on people holding to eat it .. In the year he (970), the back fastener, but he did not damage it, there was a small proportion of his sport became a tiger equipped .. In Ramadan, the year he (1073) met locusts, planting special beans, until he was almost executed .. After three years in Shaaban, he (1076), a repeated locust pandemic came in huge numbers, as the amount of sand and gravel and eat up the crops people suffered from hunger they crushed the husk * created minute An .. In the year of his birth (1146), the spread of Grado led iko in Iraq and damaged much of the country, which caused the market place ** to fall) 2 - Muhammad ibn Abd al-Malik at home in He (1127) in his book (addition to the history of al-Tabari), which deals with the disaster of the polisher that struck the Islamic world between (295 e) (907) and (367 e) (977) as follows: (And I followed the people (from Baghdad) the field was very intense it happened years he (942) and on God vulnerable when you cant experience the fact of lobster black selling every pound of dinars) So the safest people eat locusts, but I straightened it out on bread, cooked the last piece .. You may be reluctant to get away from the thought of eating locusts, especially that Islam was for him and the blessings of power to eat him .. But what about rats and cockroaches ?. Something awful, isn't it? ... Read only the following:

3 - return to Ibn al-Jawzi in the table (alter in the history of the Kings and nations) read the following text: (In the year (he) (836) and swept through the village (Iraq) a squadron of countless rats ... she went out to harvest Hunger made people eat mice, and after a year he (848), frequent breaks in the values of large (a species of insect lice) even despaired people of their yield .. But he ended the danger of the appearance of a species of bird more than a sparrow, claimed that he received lice so technically .. In the spring month the next year he (860) has an overweight of cockroaches in (Baghdad), an immeasurable preponderance, until I heard him in the night, the locusts worked with a huge sound, as if they were flying ... and onto the green land. .. and on a board for those who hunted crickets and ate them while art was not, it was poor to eat them as they are, and eat them with some kind of bread ... the haves fried them in oil.) You are disgusting to yourself. ? ... Wait a bit, focus time has not come yet .. Disgust for rats and cockroaches, so what do you get, to where will you read this? ... 4 - even with Ibn al-Jawzi in the table (enter the history of kings and peoples) read the following text: (In the year he (855), at the expense of the animals that died from her injuries, *** .. and then in the year he (938), a repetition of the epidemic in animals was all found by people by a severe drought, so they had to eat the meat of dead animals and this was the reason for the appearance of samples and blisters on the skin of people, and then this repeated in the year he (940 peace) and death in cattle and there are his people dead. In the year he (1045), a sign of an epidemic in animals, everything is so good that I did not climb on him ... twelve thousand heads perished from the king's camp (father's machine of the Seljuks) and he daily carried more than a cent of a head all over Iraq that was

put in the Tigris river until it was filled, avoiding the evil people from the water, Oman, al-Qahtani and the connection ... and that both he (1060) and he (1067) and the symptoms are usually eye puffs, head puffs, tightness in the throat, shortness of breath - and people visiting doctors because they call it barley in ode, do not work .. The spread of the epidemic to sing so that the sponsor would fly to her in the morning and find her dead. she was over five hundred years old head..as as long as the epidemic goes wild, so people had to hunt for the red monster with their own hands and then punish her. And stop the cost harsh, like for too long all animals are a feather..and meat makes people eat meat from dead animals..took many different epidemics .., Oman, then in every place) You could argue that this is nothing..I still eat carrion and shoot rodents, snakes, rabbits, live and eat them raw, but I feed on beetles and drink urine sometimes part of the training is harsh, no matter what the storm is in most armies of the state .. But if God allowed eating the falling, then he provided praise or confusion, like we all know .. I say: don't believe it ... but it doesn't concern me .. Still in the cold ... we have never had it on trials before .. I just wanted to take you gradually .. Just be patient and finish the article ... This is our plan - our first steps on this cloudy sunny day ... 5 - Male (Abu Jafar Muhammad Ibn Jarir Al-Tabari) in his book (History of the Apostles and Kings) (923), which reads as follows: (When it was emphasized that Abu Ahmed Talha the conciliator is the brother of cell culture on based on God (256-he) (870-892), screws on the owner of the Negro **** area to sit in one of the accommodations deep in the river of my father's fertile Southern Iraq in the years he (882), Interrupted by him in Almera, a kettle the price of wheat, when they caught and they ate people, and then they ate varieties of grain, and then even upwards, who followed people, if through someone a woman or a boy or a man killed him and ate him, then they became a strong man. is the time to decipher, if not, by killing him and eating his flesh and then they ate the meat of their children, then they should be dead, they reach their coffins and eat their flesh, not minding to slander anyone who did something that only guards if the match is locked) - Do you expect me to comment? Actually, I'll just say: no comment Well known so ... known for his honesty and dedication and written by many who think and say .. Someone might say that niggas are a circle of people alien to Islam, but maybe , they were not Muslims only in name, but excluded their hunger, which rose to their origins by the African customs of their ancestors in cannibalism .. And do not say: maybe you are right, but wait until you read what people are doing (Basra) while niggas surrounded by their army try to kill them, rob and burn roles ...

6 - Mention of Abu Al-Hasan Ali ibn al-Hussein Al Masawd of middle age (he) (956) in his book (Meadows of gold), which reads as follows: (And when he joined the army of the owner of the Negro (Basra) in Shawwal in the year his (871), work for the invading army among the people died and families ... gone.many of them are afraid ... they showed up, they take the dog, go to them and eat them, and the mice of the scene (cats) and did not even serve them for something .. They would be if he died from them actually ate it. Some kind of death is taken into account and how they can kill and eat its owner .. and not something from fresh water) Look what did you do to get people (Basra) Muslims .. I put them back in the folder ... and set the domain on my eyes to keep them alive. Then a real man appeared, and every human being that will manifest on the Day of Resurrection, when he says everything from himself ... to himself .. They ate dogs and cats (hooks) and even rats until the very end .. Then he got up to eat flesh of a dead man ... and not only that .. But they watched the death of some ... and this is also not easy .. They fought to kill each other Vickers her face .. Didn't I tell you that this is the law jungle? .. It was not the people (Baghdad) that so long ago ... see with me the following: 7 - mentions the house in his book (addition to the history of Al-Tabari) as follows: (Identified area of Baghdad in the year he (941), many deaths were all paid for from the mute and prayer of the people, in which religion and kindness to the living and the enveloping of the dead both emerged from another unholy evil,

where they were supposed to be graves, forcing the dead to eat their meat and their coffins .. Then befell people (Baghdad) region of another year he (946) and ate nuclear fire and is dead tsov carried, the man (focus) hit the water and remained on the floor of the rail and is under the eaten people died from the fact that people ate it was a fact of screaming: hunger, not death. And he discovered that a woman had shot a boy alive.) Therefore, the famine was made by people from (Baghdad), they eat everything ... and everything .. Starting with locusts and kernels, and this must have at least something .. We pass through rats , cockroaches and carrion, and it makes you nauseous .. But what about poop? ... What about eating the flesh of the dead ?? I What about C biology and devour them properly ??? Isn't that an incredible thing in his mind? Where then were the Muslims? .. .. But where was the mushroom from them? .. Their humanity is ?? .. Less pain for you if: Hunger is disbelief And come back, because I am in no hurry to judge grandparents .. Who knows if we lived up to their time and took us for their saints, then what will we do with time ??? Do you want the ugliest one? ... Let's then decide which plan (Masud) in the same book (Golden Meadows) is for the people (Basra) too. 8. (Al Masaud): (If you forgot that the dying woman was with her sister, and we were all waiting for her death .. What if she dies? Even a piece of her flesh, and I will never leave her sister, but her head .. So he went to cry and hurt them in her sister.) And out of the dark !! Did the sister buy her sister's hand, or her thigh, or her breasts, is that ?? !! God, God. - Asked Dora.: (Evil Scourge laughs) Do you know the most sarcastic one? He says: (It was a piece of meat) .. Then everything happened right after the slicer .. Yes, this meat was raw ... they didn't even let them cook the meat !!! Are you in your stomachs? I can see that your number has decreased more, it carried most of you and they could not continue ... did you not warn from the beginning? Of what? So I do my best to resist the nausea and she smiles even now, three pills of (death) anti-vomiting medicine so that I can complete what I am facing .. Let's ...

9-Ibn al-Jawzi in his book (regular in the history of Kings and peoples): (Signed the return of a large work in the year he (1031), what we saw as ever..so I froze the water of the tiger or almost .. . and collect wine vinegar for animals and people ... use Paternoster to stop the dead end in money and money, to open their case, and stops the wheels from spinning on the Tigris .. the wind came black very castle of crops and olive trees and date palms until i didn't rip the palm tree from her origin and then loaded the chest of her house between her and her three roles..and gouged the wind in the roofs of houses and mosques in all the villages..and the cold so weighed between pounds more.. saw that I weighed a hundred and fifty pounds, and he was asleep, and he was lowered into the ground near his hand..the extermination of cattle lasted up to six months..extermination to create a lot So I saw bodies frozen in layers, so as not to find who was paying them .. spread carnage by forcing people to eat carrion even if the technician killed his children nd values .. And, with Boulder the fight changed to not include his paper raised to slaughter him and eat him) And now it's time to kill children and eat them .. It's incredible, but it happened and it was documented historically .. Who can doubt the authenticity of the people from the cape and when is it used? I am All Trust, and all ru is an indisputable fact .. Now, what do the Iraqis have to say about grandparents? Take your time .. Before closing, I would like to remind you of this fact from the book of the most (ordinary) son of al-Jawzi. I leave after the government is completely over to you .. I wanted to finish it because this is what the variation of the total reported in this article .. I urge you, before you believe it, to admit carefully, just as long as you have picture .. And your judgment is correct ... 10-Ibn al-Jawzi in his book (regular in the history of kings and peoples): (When he signed al-Qahtani on the reign of the Abbasid caliph of fears to God in him (940) and signed in (Iraq) dear harsh until the sale of Silks what price ten dinars DHS did not find, buying it, penetrated the country until the loss of the implant and cattle, he ate people with bran and hashish, even if the technician ate them Jeff and the matches of their hands and the beasts of the Earth ... and lasted long, until renewable sources were discovered .. many of the devastation created a lot of hunger and hunger. thirst..so everyone was paid into a single grave without prayer and ablution .. and people began to eat the weak in them .. and with that fresh water .. and they were in great need of ascites, then a suitable cudgel of succession among the people came out of ascites and they went to the source of ascites not to fall. Then a month after the club of the Caliphate areas in the market, which a woman from the people (Baghdad) saw the Messenger of Allah, peace be upon him in the appropriate desert to keep the rain .. tell her to told people to fast for three days and then come out of ascites on the fourth day, God throws them with God's help ... and that's why she orders a number of people there in today's complex world of ascites after three days of fasting. They said that he started the assignment: This is suitable for a woman, And you know what an interpretation is? .. Is it right to call the caliphate to him? ... Say that we cannot format..so how are we going to live with So these people outside did not mention this product .. Formulated the people for three days to observe the order of succession to the throne, which is why on the fourth day it was Tuesday and people went out to the Egyptian sea, they fornicated .. The Omani version of rain .. Varba implanted .. and finished with hunger) I think this proves indisputably that grandparents had what they did ... and there was no awkwardness .. Their hearts were also full of faith. Didn't I tell you not to hang out around?

In the next article, we will continue the story of the disasters that have occurred in the land of Muslims throughout history and what led to this. I just went to the West for a bit. Where the gift of the Nile is. (Egypt) .. But this is not (Egypt) Pharaonic charm .. Not (Egypt) civilization sunshine .. But (Egypt) is dark .. I will take you on a night walk on the Nile. Then we walk the streets of Ancient Egypt and throughout life (customs) observe the splendor of the Fatimid architecture .. We will see things that decorate their plates with mosaics .. And arabesques that enhance mashrabiya in perfect harmony with the ivy leaves and grapes around them .. We will write on doors and walls with gold and the smell of incense, and women who are tired of this place. The image of a witch, isn't it? But we must not take sugar with us .. We must wait for a good share of the middle of the street and avoid the sword next to the house, just stay that celandine ... Yes, hooks hanging from the roofs of those houses that differ from each other by the tail of bad luck Sha ability walking around these houses, only to end up in the stomach of the hungry, who replaced them. Kakhtani is facing loss .. But this is another article by the will of God. As long as you're okay ...

1.we are people just like people, and what relates to people is applicable 2 - you must freeze from whims when you read such articles, which do not even differ from identical constructions of judgments 3 - we should have more information about the history of our new history that we have in our own ignorance

And today we are here together, we are using this series of articles .. Today we will talk about (Egypt) .. I believed (Herodotus) (1) when he said that these eternal beauties: (Egyptian gift of the Nile) .. Research in freedom will reveal that this country is committed throughout history, closely associated with the radical and with the Nile River. When the good should be several hundred ... declaring (Egypt) back .. and prosperity .. When it recedes prevails in communion and throughout the country .. Such is the history of (Egypt) .. Closely associated with this river began from the very beginning of creation. .and will not end until it becomes the same value .. Since the economy (of Egypt) was primarily agricultural, the economy was critically dependent on irrigation from the water of the Nile, he says (otter) (2) tell him (Yakut al-Hamawi) (3) in your book (lexicon of countries): (And miracles (Egypt) .. Nile .. make it so that God does not give water for growth and does not sing praise to rainwater) And without the ado, let's get into the topic directly. Today's topic of the day is really long, despite my tireless search for the shortest path possible .. So let's get the story straight ...

The earliest Muslim Arabs conquered Egypt, they are aware that it is large and abundant .. There is no doubt that Islamic Egypt should have enjoyed a significant part of the wealth and prosperity while it was not - according to 'Amr ibn al -As - an amendment to the caliphate as a whole, named by some mistakes that: (basket version) Since it was no longer faithful to the closet .. But the prosperity of Egypt was not spared from some economic crises that from time to time cut the rope of this prosperity .. Hit the conclave (4) when he said in his book (the best of decrees in the battle for territories) from Egypt: (This territory, if you accept, do not ask for a breeding license, and if the driest god of drought is now) Says Makrisi (5) in your book (relief of the nation, reveal all): (Not only economic crises in Egypt in the Islamic period of its history without others, but there is this crisis in all epochs of the history of Islamic Egypt: the era of birth ... the era of toluene, the era seed, then the Fatimid period) It should be noted here that the prevalence of what we know about the polishing areas that occurred in the Fatimid period does not necessarily mean that the age was the worst, but that it was due to the fact that what was said came to us from history and what struck Egypt in other times .. Let's go back and say that the stability of the Fatimid dynasty in Egypt and the survival over a long period of time of such as Abbasid Baghdad, make historians strive to document the disasters that befell Egypt in that era .. Before we can talk about the disasters and economic crises that hit Egypt, let's first look at their causes .. The main reason, as I said, is the Nile. life in Egypt was and will still be associated with the Nile River:

1.   Nile spill:

Irrigation in Egypt, the old CF basin depends on the Nile flood, so stylists have strived since antiquity to create bays and canals, and it was there that there were 7 bays before the Islamic conquest of

Egypt: Generous Bay, Damietta Bay and Exile Bay, Bay Area and Narrative Virus Bay. the bay of Alexandria .. In the bay of the warlord of the faithful, a new hole 'Amr ibn al -' Aas appeared in his first stay in Egypt, to deliver the world to the people of the Hejaz, in the famous of which there was ash .. In the Islamic era, the flat of the bays of others like the bay dad recuperator who is best preserved bin Badr each in the continuity of the suspension depends on God Fatimid year he is down on the advice of my father recuperator Ben Chaya Jewish source .. Then they built dams on nozzles of bays and canals before the flood was taken by the allies, clay, and they built a dam after another, turned off the irrigation already in stages. Then they built bridges to save water from the flooding of shops, to organize the irrigation process .. Says Nasir Khusraw (6) Persian traveler who visited Egypt during the reign of Al-Mustansir Billah of the Fatimids in his book (seat): (Photographers set on the beach from the first birth to the last bridge of clay, to relieve people of the secret treasury of the Sultan every year by ten thousand dinars, to update the building and maintenance .. It was for Egypt according to the recipe at all balls, it was one hundred twenty thousand people, with them cadastral machines work all year round ... allocates them seventy thousand level five thousand down to the ground (face-Sea) and their pits bays, bridges, arches and fill with soil and cut out history and A and take measures harmful to the Earth, the government has implemented in this regard about a third of the country's remote regions, an increase in costs if the work is done.) This meant that the stylists took care, led by the Nile spill, to provide access to agricultural land and on the other hand predict Besny tensile strength and prosperity they are so metrics are numerous along the course of the river in the lower part of the Earth (Delta) at the highest (level) .. and the column of the Marble set is divided into hands and fingers, and months, which scales scale (exile) .. It was necessary to irrigate the land to reach level 14 the hand lined up to be called abruptly enough .. and it was in the reign of the Fatimid dynasty, but the most suitable decoder for prosperity 16 hand lined up to be called sharply clear, but the degree of flooding decoder 18 hand lined up to be called sharply clear .. that threatens the flooding of cities and flooding .. It should be noted that the lack of Nile water not only reflected on irrigation and agriculture, but also not the worst effect on domestic trade, which depended mainly from the Nile River in the transport of goods between parts of the country .. It is the lack of Nile water that gives the biography of Lod ok, as it happened in that year when the lack of water in the Nile was a big drawback of Yahya ibn Said of Antioch (7) in his book (reference to the history of Asia): (Now the Nile has locked up its animals this led to the disruption of the boats at sea to east of the camp .. This was given to boats - of course - threatens to reduce the cost in the big cities of the castings, which were considered in Merton for what happens to the territories and activities of internal trade ..) This is also confirmed by what is mentioned in the papyrus of Arab papyri collected Professor Henrik puppy (8) .. It was a papyrus that lost the first wave of the initial up to the owner of the office in the wheat field in the year he calls from the point of view of that letter, the owner of the place that steals the introduction of wheat into Fustat not even to boil the price of it and tells him that it frees up the business office for wheat in order to encourage them to speed up to enter the city. This, in any case, indicates that the disabled wheat trade led to deaf prices and restrictions on the economic crisis, which is the same as it happens if the boats are given away due to the lack of the Nile waters. Not only have there been economic crises due to the lack of a Nile garden, thirst or drought, but there have also been some crises in the case of a star, caused by an excessive rise in the water level of the Nile. He speaks of Antioch:

(Where there are places that the last water presence on Vivo was the time for their planting ... it was pretty clear if the Nile occupied a quarter of the country's agricultural land, and if the planning for an eighteen cubit increase was a consequence of a pandemic perspective ..) Here shows a psychological factor that controls access to them forever in the treatment of constructors .. This is fear of tomorrow, or as it is also called ... sensor .. When people felt that they did not reach the Nile limit for a meeting or during political unrest and transmission authorities from state to state, they were used to store grain, leading to a celebration of the high cost, he says to Makrisi: (People were always there, if they stopped, then the Nile on the days of his visit increased or slightly decreased himself speaking after the dawn of the Nile, they took cereal with their own hands and please sell it at a high price and scenes of money in a safe income, either ask for a price, or order them to spare the strength of their children, then Yes, this is a price increase, an increase in the price of dissolved water otherwise it was a meager drought, in maintaining the growth of public interest and, yes, vice versa) In short, there were two sessions takes two in Egypt and causes what is in hunger:

A, - on: (the arrival on the Nile of a pretty pretty one - people are afraid and keep grain - death of crops and the lack of internal trade - increase in prices - death of livestock or slaughtered livestock - getting rid of the burden of satisfaction and eating its meat - drought GDP is possibly accompanied by an epidemic - multiplication of death -the revolution of the hungry and eat carrion and the dead-government intervention multiplying bakers and greed and laws and out of my grain-the dissolution of the crisis) B-oh: (the arrival of the Nile is pretty clear-the flooding of plantations and the financial-cost of the pandemic and the reproduction of death ...)

2-animal husbandry:
It was the flood of the Nile that caused the decomposition of pastures and a lack of forage, leading to massive deaths of livestock, as well as its sometimes plague deaths where meat is impossible. As for the presence of movement of agricultural land, there is no need to talk about this ..

3 - agricultural pests:

Whether agricultural pests were the causative factors of economic crises in Islamic Egypt, it is these pests that receive the harvest that falls on most of these pests: A-rat: B. Locusts: Where there were locusts and mice, a frightening costume date increases in several years on all plantations ..

4 - a epidemic, plague:

Makrisi says: (The epidemic often began in a rapidly developing population, especially in the city of Fustat, their poor social conditions and health, it was Fustat that was the center of a crowded population, the most severe congestion and its streets are narrow and arranged raise their legs, descend from it again and because of his air makes him this bad air accumulates vulnerable to an epidemic that spreads among people at a speed due to narrow streets and overcrowding in the city, for this was pleasing to the residents of the city fleeing to the countryside from the epidemic, if Fustat's decision)

5.trust and

6 - internal and external attacks:

Where people save their plagues with them, when they fled from them both from Fustat in the territory and vice versa, or from tea, Iraq and Egypt at that time there was no one familiar with the concept of quarantine and travel ... with a note on the increase in population as a result of migration to Egypt caused hunger ..

7 - fake money !!

8-fires.

9 earthquake.

Now with an overview of some of the epidemics and famines that have occurred in Egypt throughout its Islamic history:

1-era states: (21-on / 641 - 868 world):
Sawiris Ibn Mukaffa says (9) in his book (History of the Patriarchs): (What happened in him in the state of Abdullah ibn Abi Sarh did not happen dear, like that time goes on in those days when every level in the village is required for the yield, and there are more people in streets and markets, like the dead, like the sky of the city photo on puddles of water, and a large number die every day) Makrizi says: (In 66, a plague began in Egypt, and he died in a great creation .. In the year 70, the plague was signed by the last epidemics in Egypt in the state Abdul Aziz bin Marwan came out Abdulaziz Al-Fustat on the run to Helwan that he liked the contact on housing and make war and help .. If Abdul Aziz escaped the epidemic he had the opportunity to die in an epidemic in another inn in Fustat was also a year he .. in the year 87 e Gar Nil is only a thing .., Oman, the high cost, and that after nine years in the reign of Abdallah ibn Abd al-Malik ibn Marwan was the brunt of the great search for compatible people son 'Abd al-Malik heard his Makkesson and in ultimately with the departure of Abdullah from Egypt to Safar next year's notice he curses the hybrid poets .. In the year he is mandated by the decision of the American bar Inn country B great and dead every day does not know their number frequent to them. In the 96th year, taking control of the remote regions of Egypt, Osama bin Zayed wrote to the Umayyad Caliph Suleiman bin Abdul Malik that: (Peach even keep the location, and then blood until it swells) Wounding the people of Egypt with great fury and choosing the high price of the Great Death, because he created much more than died in a pandemic .. In 105, in the state of Muhammad ibn Abd al-Malik, his brother Hisham took place in Egypt, a strong epidemic fled from Muhammad ibn Abd al-Malik to the level, but returned a few days later to Fustat to get out of Egypt

never get distracted, only about a month. In 108 year E in the state of Hafs ibn Al-Walid in Egypt, according to Hisham ibn Abd al-Malik, a severe drought happened in Egypt, which passed my exam for ... they went out to pray Muslim dropsy, which they wrote, fornication, thank God .. In 133 E in the state of Papa's help from the first era of Abbasids up the Nile towards my class of people prayers for rain came out that Muslims, Jews and Christians from the people of Fustat and Giza .. and the high cost of a severe epidemic, he fled from Abu Aun to Damietta , fearing an epidemic ..) ....

2.   tulunid state: (he / 868 world-on 904 world)
It is worth noting that the Tulunid era in Egypt was an era of economic prosperity, not seen by Egypt during any crisis or this or that area as a result of the good governance of Ahmed Ibn Tulun and the recent political and economic crisis. I remember in this era that who has a strong earthquake in Egypt, and about the rarity of earthquakes in Egypt, but it was very intense..my son says path (10) in his book (substance system) Famous b (my path): (In the reign of care in 273 e there was a great tremor in Egypt, the role landed and many died to create a lot ... people thought that he would shake an hour, settle down, they, Oman, the author of the high cost, even the price of D wheat (13) DT ... and learned boots even to eat flaxseed people ... died to create a lot, even filled the markets of Egypt, the dead carried them to everyone according to all the sentences of the eight dead and brought them to dig up their great casting) .. Like what happened in the 290s from Al -Kah Thani, the way out of the unprofitable flood level is far enough. carving out the diameter of the sky, there were droughts for 3 years, so that drier ones ended with the fall of the Tulunid general 292 E and the return of Egypt under Abbasid rule again, and remained so for three decades .. Son of the virgins of Marrakech (11) in his book (exposition of Morocco in the selection of the history of the Kings of Al-Andalus and Morocco): (It happened in 307 A.D. in the state of Zaki, the one-eyed ruler of Egypt, the Abbasid caliph of God

Muktadir, so that Goleta prices in Egypt and stop the epidemic in people and it is clear that many of them and they were on their flight from the epidemic they carry with them when the sweet spreads overflow the epidemic across the country even spent two-thirds of the population .. During this there was no drought in Egypt, but because of the revolution of Muhammad bin Ali in the Persian Gulf on the corrupt to the ruler of the Abbasids Muhammad ibn Suleiman, the author of the harassment from the family of lengths the..as the result of this confidence communicates how serious..and the country as a whole .. Then take Egypt Wali Hilal bin Bader (309 - 311 e) settle the conditions of Egypt and many dead people in the people and corruption and cut the way home the source of the Great on the coming of the poor Crescent to reform the conditions of Egypt, so whenever the dam is going to get it back his days in Egypt were evil days, so why aggravate it with an isolated cell culture capable of God. The wall changed, and the affair that followed Mohammed with acid in the entry of Fustat in the year he / 935 ... the foundation of the state ultimately ..)
....

2-ultimately: (he / 935 world-he / 960)
It all started with locusts, he says to his son.: (In the year when he attacked Egypt, the Crayfish in their countless numbers prevented even the sun's ray from falling to the ground, and he stepped on the vines, fruits, bran, even ruined gardens and fields. .Oman was starving and the people went out in their request to eat to the end .. In those years he saw a dish of crayfish in Egypt, and he came to all the crops and trees ... and the past was permeated by the free, the most speaking first and informed people that they were they ate from their uncle from everywhere ... he ate people, animals from the streets, and then they ate Jeff for the last time.) Then it happened to pass by the rats of Egypt, he says to Makrisi: (Signed in 341, the rat destroyed the yield and chrome .. and choose a severe hunger that made people eat dogs and cats and then rats..and some trustworthy that rat-catching was easy for monstrosity there

was a mouse equivalent to the size of a rabbit ..) Then there was a fire next to the famous ... said son virgins: (Big - for big fires a year he's in the reign of camphor seed the Great Fire of Fustat took place in the market of the guild of merchants of Caesarea honey entered the night fire, the situation did not change and patted the people for danger Great therefore Cavour ordered to call: (who came closer or because the water would not be AED) They turned off the amount of ten thousand odd dirhams, and these were, among other things, non-food products, fabrics and sixteen thousand houses) Then Egypt is going through the most serious economic crises and throughout its history during the reign eventually ... I heard that the crisis nine whole years, where I started the year he describes it said maqrizy: (Then the signed high cost in the end, also lasted nine years, consecutive beginning in the year fifty-two, three hundred and the prince, as the memory of Ali ibn Ahmad ibn destroy things for my father, musk, camphor acid was the reason for the high cost that the water of the Nile ended its visit at five, ten cubits and four fingers from the price after the license I mouth was for one became three Dinars, the experience is attributed, why there is an increased high cost, while wheat is all and (14) in the palace D of the Nile in the year fifty-three, only fifteen cubits four fingers were reported and the boats increased once the transmission again until it was half a month from the door to the close of thirteen cubits, and then increased a little and quickly, the high cost and density of the business period The looted losses or harvests and magic people in Egypt because of the price, and they entered the antique side of Fustat on Friday jammed when students died a man and a woman in the crowd and before everyone on that day and avoid expensive years he and the level of impact of the attack a spell that even reached akhmīm..The quarrels between Abu al-Hasan Ali ibn Ahmad ibn al-Hasan Egypt and camphoric acid in his kingdom even prevented the camphor people from meeting and resolved the dispute only after the death of Abu al-Hasan Ali in 355 AD of Van Camphor by Egypt. In the fifty-fifth year, the sum of the increase was fourteen cubits and fingers and the palace for a while, and I said that I ruled it in the fifty-sixth year, I did not reach the Nile, only a dozen cubits and fingers and the like in Jamia Millia Islamia and there was the command of Egypt then camphor seed great command of the severity of the high cost .. Then Matt camphor and took Abu al-Favoris Ahmad ibn Ali Seed is the son of 11 years. This was made difficult by the situation of the country upset her period and the wars between the soldiers and princes behind her sacrifice created a lot with the markets lit a fire and doubled the price before selling in (15) wheat six dinars for high prices even call it expensive, great. People ate carrion and dogs .. and they fall dead of hunger and therefore the Great Epidemic from what was done to the burial of the dead, decoding encourages them to dig and where a lot of their soil does not harden and does not wash and does not shroud the dissenting military, he followed many of them the garden of ibn Abdullah ibn IS that day in the sands and complete many of them Al-Muizz li Din Allah the Fatimid greatness of the area with the report of the karmati to Egypt there were frequent news of the arrival of the soldiers of the goat of Morocco will be introduced in fifty-eight, three hundred and entered the commander of the essence the Sicilian militarization of Imam Al-Muizz li Din Allah .. And further, like the record that took into account IP prices .. was struck by the beauty of flour, two and tender with them ... and brokers collect crops in one place and do not exchange crops only there, and does the office at home one way of decoding does not come out a bowl of wheat (16) only and Suleiman-bin-definition of an accountant and continued to grow until a year or six cases in which the epidemic consumed disease and death, so that I The people could not envelop the dead and push them to unscrew them from the dead knocking on the Nile .. When he entered the sixty-first year at the lowest price in which he used the land and received wealth, I sold every nine cups of wheat for a denarius). ....

3.   Fatimids: he / 973 peace - he / 1171 peace

The entry of the essence of Sicilian Egypt into it in the midst of the economic crisis that overturned Palestine was a gutter affair ... I thought maybe for the first time in Islamic history money counterfeiting !! .. it was a Dinar counterfeit !! .. Makrizi says :(The year it appeared in Egypt, the so-called White Dinar (meaning fake) and was worth ten studies, the authorities could not interfere with the trade, so the essence of the Sicilian reduction in its value was that the six client communication studies and creation were many. also mention the occurrence of the Great Pandemic, the Egyptian in he..so that almost Egypt from the economic crisis, which took away pieces so suffered..Makrizi says: (The year he bought the epidemic of diseases in Cairo..the tide of the pandemic is a great degree violence from people who could not envelop the dead and bury them, they knocked their dead into the Nile, there is no doubt that people who sinned in the right of the dead returned to them in more communication, which led to the transmission of infection and the spread of the epidemic..technically half of the population of Egypt. The Fatimids themselves were at the beginning of their beginning of the welfare and prosperity of Egypt by the statesmanship of Al-Muizz li Din Allah, and after the dear son of God in fulfilling the conditions of parishioners and economic reforms ... and passed the period of their sentences without crises, but the uncle flourished in the country, and remember, that in the era of a powerful god, the high cost of years followed, he had a cruel epidemic in Egypt, spent many countless of them, continued this epidemic even exceeding the next year .. Then he took the situation at the behest of God - this is the son of 11 and a half years .. And in the reign of his miracles for disrespect, the soldiers got out of control and tried to prove their honesty on the other hand ... It prohibited the sale of a bottle-drink made of barley - Malv's thermos and fish that did not clean it and did not hit it on the neck .. Banned the sale of raisins and banned trade on a trip to Egypt, and then collect a large amount that I burned on the banks of the Nile, was spent on cremation only without a cost of five hundred dinars and sold it to grapes, and cut the vines, and burned what was in the honey reserves, broke the pots and the heart of the Nile until it was full, raised the excise tax on the crops, then gave it back, and then picked up some and kept others ... and manipulated The government for the coin classes with new ones and ordered the people to replace them with the old ones is what caused the government to lose control over the people, equivalent to 60% of the true value of their money..also included the grain trade ministers and came in prices to achieve higher profits ..the epidemic of high prices followed in the years when he and many people of Egypt continued to spread until recently. Over the years he was growing with diseases attributed to drugs and many others ..) As the son of Aibak (12) in his book (the name sounded in the plans for the next) year, he: (Eat a rat in Egypt, until he came to them, of course, was the destruction of crops leads to an increase in the prices of the remaining and shows the high cost in addition to this, it is the mice that save the plague and lead to outbreaks that threaten a large number of people and livestock, which should have led to the emergence of fields ..) This is in addition to the revolution, Pope Recco Umayyad sites on Fayoum..my son says APIK: (The revolution was the source of domains throughout the history of Egypt, for example, the revolutionary pope. Recco Al-Walid ibn Hisham, an Umayyad who came out of the Fayum aspects, in the succession of Hakim Fatimid settled price problems or exorbitant lack of experience and a shortage of flour, and people with money ties and tough financial conditions intervened in what the authorities would like to tighten on the market: (Any price increase stipulates that the same murder lowered the price alone) ..) In addition, the palaces due to the flooding of the Nile led to drought and exorbitant prices in price .. Makrizi says: (The price of a Dinar is up to 34 dirhams .. wheat all seems to be four dinars and rice is all it seems dinars and beef, one and a half pounds for dirhams lamb, pound (17) dirhams, onions and ten pounds for dirhams and then my ace (18) dirhams and eat eight for dirhams ... flour, pound in..and all two pounds for dirhams and a quarter, and the poor and needy find that to feed their children only coarse cauliflower, which went to the shops for cabbage heads and sprinkle them with the Vega of the poor with a little cabbage. earn almonds and earn sesame seeds .. lasts or an exorbitant salary of water for animal feed and the absence falls on us by the sale of the novel beautiful three studies the mule storyteller rejoices and the patients of the torment they paid for grinding the hive five studies .. It lasts or prohibitively kattan whole grains and decide for the harm of eating .. many cases of marade rstations were carried out by slaves of the state and some of the carts, so they plundered the city of Ashmun and then plundered the coast of Fustat, opening schools, the parents of them went and faced them in several facts and closed many shops, some roles and years were freed, and in in most forms of communication, they were free. Then the experience and learned the boots .. and the past and slags disappeared . store grain and sell it on the black market .. overfill the board and often die as a result of malnutrition and create a lot of hunger .. and leaving the Caliphate in your cortege find the essence of the people you missed to rummage around with the exception of the guards who were able to sneak it into the palace and chant: (Hunger, hunger..so what did your father and your grandfather do.) He ordered the Khalifa to hit each of the grain warehouses in the neck, vacate the house and loot his money..he was afraid of tanks from the accountant up to 150 storing a secret warehouse of wheat. But what, when they passed it like that .. Then they ordered to kindly mill the laws, so they were beaten with whips in the field and for a month ... they solved the crisis a little. In the year when he increased the Nile, a significant increase in planning is quite clear even sinking traffic jams filled all the place of the base money was left through the delivers available only from the desert sank lost gardens ..) Then he took the phenomenon of soldiers of the religion of Allah changed his father to the situation in 414 was the first to pass laws to reduce the mortality of the past, such as a ban on the slaughter of women..and the slaughter of cows and sound that are suitable for this event..and fines, fines, and sometimes on violators .. And in his reign a terrible epidemic that swept Egypt throughout the decoder is a similar epidemic that occurred in the days of the Sicilian entity .. Makrisi says:

(In the phenomenon of the continuity of the soldiers of the religion of Allah Fatimid, there is a big difference between illness and death in people in the year when he created people, which of the B About the celebration of Christmas Eve and the frequency of the epidemic and so it was not without a home is one of a number of patients, the spread of the epidemic in oasis years he herds of the family chickenpox the great died out, creating many people, then the people of Egypt rebelled, epistaxis the Great in the same year he concluded the phenomenon of succession Bob another decision of the Egyptian years he did not live the phenomenon after he died long ago in half of the Shaaban year he ..) He then took over the government of Mustansir Billah in him after the death of his father of the phenomenon..it is the seventh son of his age. his reign has witnessed the harshest and most brutal events that have taken place over Egypt throughout its history, but I will not mention anything about it now, but I will not wave my hand, you will see how you persecute him, it is worth it to talk about it in detail .. Then he adopted the succession of suspension depends on God, who succeeded his father, Al-Mustansir, and there was an earthquake two strong in Egypt for two consecutive years AMI 487 one at the level of his succession, destroying the role of many technicians to create a lot and came next and ruins .. Then he led the caretaker to the provisions of the Caliphate .. UAL Best bin Badr also has a weight behind his father's back. My son says to the virgin Marrakech: (During the mandate of the keeper of the provisions of God, Mansour happened in the year when he is an epidemic following the cost of this year, and then renewed the next year he died creating many in 493 uncles over the country of plague as a result of this delegation to Egypt, a large number of the population of the Levantine country avoided the Frankish attacks of the crusaders on the screen, and they carried the epidemiology to overwhelm the epidemic of the country and died in Egypt created a lot) .. Says Makrisi: (In a year he is from wheat in Egypt, then Hannah selling the first hundred to a hundred thirty dinars so the best Commander Abdullah bin you missed - a step after this sale of Mammon - the Wall of calculation in order to measure the sealing of the risk of yields and brought their fathers well-being, to keep their crops under the seal, to give a new or issued and every STO at thirty dinars, the answer was issued and sold at the indicated price and the seal on the coefficients must be kept, provided that people need every day the grain yield, which the trade responded to sell at the assigned price what is needed then the sale of ultra-Sai flour for two the same price..so also what should be introduced gives new decided prices..The owners were forced to give in stored to sell it out of fear of licorice, sold it for a little regret that they had missed out of the house at the first price .. That year he infused a black wind to Egypt and continued for three days the face of many people and animals Admi damaged plantings and cultures .. Revealed in the sequence of necessity for the religion of Allah Abdul Majid more economic crisis first occurred between the years he-Ah 532 was at the cost of outrageous how bad ... but he did not continue the best that he galloped towards ancient Egypt and brought all the related claims income and literature a group of monopolists and price hikes hired them to do what he needed every day to beat him himself and took him right .. otherwise it's still a matter of that the God of prosperity, revealing that the people of their TIN of communication .. Then an epidemic occurred, in one year he suffered greatly, and the greatness of the next year even perished in countless creation .. In Shaaban of the same year, the yield of prices for both wheat and barley rose wheat ninety dirhams in flour, one hundred fifty in campaign (mobile), bread, three pounds for the DHS logo seven site studies, butter, nutmeg, a pound for three studies and every pound for DHS and all one hundred and ten studies, hot oil a pound rejoices and one and a half Taro every pound rejoices and the broiler chicken does not offer anything superfluous to an adult .. Alternately, the winner in the victory of God in the year he signed the cost of the service of the good pioneers of the USA, the disaster was in wheat, five dinars of insufficient Nile water to fulfill the supply of crops countless among many grain and its flour, two and the cheapest prices and the prevention of monopoly and ordered people to sell existing ones and comment on the beauty of the poor often and princes and the sides on the left and the same about the people where they were from communication was quickly dissolved by the crisis, Oman and prosperity .. Well-established pioneers of American catastrophic potential in managing the affairs of the Fatimids .. Why the murder worsened the conditions for the succession of the Fatimids and before God the last successors of the Fatimids and the termination the conflicts famous among the Schauers were on the negative Egypt became a field for the Crusades, which led to the intervention of Nur ad-Din Mahmud in turn, to pay the crusaders for the capture of Egypt, battles fell and wars were undeniably the worst blow to the country's economy and Fustat signed the prey of this conflict with then moved on to a manual shower, which was burned to the ground so that it would not fall into the hands of the crusaders, so the country suffered. from the economic crisis, chronic in these conditions, political consequences can explain to us the satisfaction of the people with the fall of the Fatimids at the hands of Saladin and their satisfaction with this source that it turned out so it was said: He did not enter it in the fall, he used two goats ..)

but after the technician there is already my quiver with arrows or almost .. Those arrows that lie on the streets and in shops are either dead or suffering in death throes. Without what you discover when you pay for it, not because of the lack of funeral, but because of the lack of opportunity to be buried, it is technically different. He was just lucky that they died at the Yard comprehensively, that they found themselves transporting their bodies in the mosque to him, and then paying for him .. Or to wear the Nile when I often visit the central waters, in its darkness .. What important, because it's straightforwardness .. Either buried, or buried money. It may sound ugly, but the most disgusting is keeping your body out in the open but buried. You are not afraid of anything, it will not be a body, but a restaurant for the stage, technically this is so .. Under Ashraf, the stylists announced the disappearance of the very existence of the faculty .. When the history of Ashraf erases the name of Egypt from its pages .. A hand stretched out by the gracious Dhuhur after the skinny one. .. are after torment .. He brought Egypt back to a new life .. Today we will talk about almost the same events .. But in another place ... not far from Egypt. At that time she was in Algeria. I love God's country with all my heart after Egypt. Before I start the article, let's ask a question that has haunted me since childhood: Why is Algeria called that way ?? Strange question, but the strangest thing is the marking is the same..it is not the Islands, do you understand something? ... I mean, the island, also known from the books of geography throughout history, is a piece of land surrounded by water on all sides .. This does not apply to Algeria .. Digging deeper, I was able to find the answer ..

Historical sources say that Belkin Ben Zerah founded the Zirid dynasty in Algeria when he founded his capital on the ruins of the Roman city of reasons (Ikosios) It was named the islands of the son of the sun because of the presence of 4 small islands near the sea coast near the city, which was confirmed by geographers -Muslims such as Yakut al-Hamawi .. The Ottomans are named Algeria on the country page of the name of the capital .. And the whole history of this country will know exactly what I say when I say that it is (the land of martyrs) .. If we want to ask history about this country ... a stretching story, "his lips said pitifully: (The troubles that befell this country are the ones that make me think about buying a chypre ..) As if those who were there did not give the people of this country an opportunity for nothing but to meet them face to face .. They were not annoyed with only one and their that the most difficult of which happened ... the most cruel of them soft .. So it is not surprising two things: First, not created to create a great civilization like the civilization of Egypt or Iraq. Secondly, the fact is that this country has the smallest number in terms of population density compared to area .. Not because of the lack of integration and development, but because the number of deaths exceeded the number of births several times. And to indicate this, we will quote the plan of the French themselves with what they did during the occupation of Algeria .. The rebellious occupation army, many of the crimes against the civilian population, which he called by historians, was (Franz .: Razzias): Says the military historian Charles André Julien (Charles A. Juliane): (Al-Razi, as the French call him, is not intended to punish the wicked, but rather became a source to empower the army ... these were all the things he sold that offered a price to the officers and soldiers, about a quarter of the officers' loot and half for everything else in the army's treasury, and the distribution of packers will be a way to change the region and did not spare it not to people and things, the generals of the African army they do not burn the hidden country. they do it and count their Glory, be it a royalist or a republican or a Haitian Bonaparte) Says the military historian dor (Ducros): (What is the booty in (Razia) one cargo of 2000 mules)

See Colonel Montana you (Montagnac) In your diary: (Some soldiers tell me to their officers, urging them not to leave anyone alive among the Arabs, all military officers who had the honor to command their troops were afraid if they would bring a cart alive to whip .. I destroyed the general lease (La Moricière) From the presence of twenty-five villagers at the exit of one it is rather a lack of humanity .. As soon as you localize, it seems, even the beginning of the rest of the soldiers to meet her and we have tents, that the health of its population depends on the approaching soldiers, so they throw women, children and men with herds of cattle in all directions, this soldier kills a sheep, one of the soldiers enters and leaves the tents, carrying carpets on their shoulders, someone carries a chicken ... they set fire to everything, they notice people and animals in the midst of the conflict and get sick, women are roaring, this is deafening vanity .. (center of the camp on December 19, 1841) .. Then he returns and says: (The general attacks the Arabs and abducts them all: women, children and cattle ... and the walking cloth holds some of their hostages, while other horses, and the rest are sold at auction like animals, their beauty, the share of officers .. (Camp March 31, 1843) .. On another page we find it written: (Women and children of refugees will not surrender to the dense grasses themselves ... they will kill ... they will kill ... the clash of victims will declare that the final mixture of animal sounds, that the borders of Targu are all going from all sides ... this is a damn specific center of ice piles, if these processes, which we did for four months, are pathetic even in the rocks, and he did not have time to take pity, but we were dealing with an inadvertently thrown atrium while cooling (camp March 31 1842) ..) The deputy speaks about the parliamentary instrument (Tocqueville): (We make more barbarians than the Arabs themselves. I did not listen as the French defeated the Iraqi war, defeating them with destruction and hunger) Says the captain, Lafaye (Lafaye): (The officers gave a choice, the peasants who brought them food or genocide ... we were in a camping next to the village, gives them a common Hey, cook food or we were aiming weapons towards the village and waiting for us then eggs await us, fresh world of fairy tales fat chicken their beautiful best sweet very masculine .. (Tlemcen 17 July 1848) .. We burned down the village of the tribe, built for year..our soldiers did not retreat to kill old people, women and children..the most cruel thing is that women are killed after being raped, but we didn't stick in front of groups, and these Arabs have nothing to defend themselves with (December 23, 1948) ..) Post Officer Tarnaue In his diary: (The country between them is really big, but we burned everything, destroyed everything, uh, from the war ... how many women and children fled in the snow of the atlas, and then died of cold and hunger (Tlemcen 17 April 1842) .. We destroy ... we ... s we finish ... we leave the house ... and we pull out the fruit-bearing tree (June 5, 1841) .. I am at the top of my army, making doir and huts and devastating al-matzamir of grain ... and at our posts in (full) wheat and barley (October 5, 1842) ..) General tenant in his diary: (..the next day, going down to the (benign) burning of everything in my path..I destroyed this lovely village..stack of bodies adjoining the body with other dead owners froze..bringing the morning, snow glued them together ... these are the people of Brown's supporters. these are the ones who burned their villages and watered them in front of the ostrich ... it was exciting (February 28, 1843) ..) And the general changed (Changarnier) in his diary: (If this happens under the direct leadership of Pogo, as a result of which his soldiers killed a dozen old women, but they defend themselves .. (Algeria, Algeria, October 18, 1841) ..) And general care (Canrobert) :) Our soldiers spent this measure of protection, if the consequences catastrophe, this act of barbarism and vandalism, a deep moral that is broadcast in the hearts of our soldiers when they kill and rape and each of them is terrible for his own personal .. (forget July 18, 1845) This is exactly what happened in Algeria during the days of the French occupation. Now do you understand why I called Algeria, a country with a population of one and a half million people, a martyr? ... This number is too high, no doubt .. But this is in modern history .. What about ancient history? this? ... And the art of Algeria, as old as the art of their recent time? ... The answer in a nutshell, unfortunately, yes, but technically I have much, much more .. Algeria all old interests of an orphanage is her more frequent visits than any other place in the world ... and you need to destroy them in many areas, not just in the article regarding the numbered pages .. So I decided that the test should focus on only one part of the story of this country and what happened to it. And let's leave you to deal with the rest of the history of Algeria .. So what happened in each era was not much different from what happened in her kiss or in the next ... - and if what we got from him is a little sad. Even this seemed like a legacy to me for generations that did not understand the meaning of scrub and peace of mind throughout the history of this great country .. You may encounter many rulers and states from the beginning of the Islamic era to the present day. Since the income of Islam from Imam Abdul-Rahman ibn Rustam, the founder of the state treasury, in it I began to call Al-Rostamani, then El-Idrissia, then the majority,

then the Al-Fatimid state ... the state of the Zirid dynasty, then the Hammadids, and then the Almohad state ... the state see the end of the Ottoman rule ... passing through it to save the Spaniards and then the French .. Long history is no doubt .. It is with this length that is filled .. So, as I said, I finished overview of this story. And what I would like to outline is the fidgeting that happened to Tlemcen during the reign of Az-Zayani (698-on / 1299-1442). When the control state of Xi'an was being built in Morocco in the Middle East or in what is now Algeria ... Wat Tlemcen was the capital of civilization by his artfully crafted borders of his state, stretching from Egypt in the east to the Atlantic Ocean in the West and the Mediterranean Sea in the north to the borders of Central Africa in the south, and affecting the lives of almost one hundred and twenty-five thousand inhabitants .. What have you done, who is this? ... This is what we will learn in a few years ...
Before we can fidget, let's first how we can cause .. The reasons that were the leading men and communities in the Middle East Maghreb are as follows:

1 - dehydration:

Poor rainfall is normal in that place on Earth and people were dying from dehydration of store supplies..they on a face that lasted for years, like two years of drought, which led to the council as a social event (303-he) and a year (776-he), as if the drought lasts three years, which is inevitably a disaster, since it was the implementation of provisions and savings and a rise in prices .. Ibn Khaldun (1): (Nature in the world often rains and I told her differently and he adds, and often planting fruit and putting pressure on the rate only that people are confident in reimbursement of needs, if you have lost respect for the greatness of people stopped Physalis Council dear ..)

2 - storms with hail:

Strong storms occurred at the end of each autumn during the winter, damaging crops and killing animals and people, as happened in (he / 1280 world) Ibn Khaldun says: (The wind was east, Morocco has long been like six months and a great pestilence and many diseases) Storms were always accompanied by cold and snow ... but in many ways it often turned into destructive typhoons .. He stated that his son Marzuk (2): (This concerned most of the Maghreb and the average cold, and strong winds, especially coming from the south, led to the burning of crops and council as a public event he / 1374, where famine was caused by a hurricane of great pain for the inhabitants of Tlemcen)

3 - floods:

Was caused by torrential rains that led to the prevention of war, seeds, destruction of crops and it was this rain that fell on the Pope, the denominator of the Fatimid months and the placing on the market of Ibrahim of the year (he / 997) not only the seriousness of the incorrect registration of this in Seoul, but and in preparing the land to avoid epidemics, that the fall of the airport after a period of drought or at an untimely time leads to the appearance of some epidemics in this regard, reminiscent of Hasan al-Wazzan (3): (In some years it rains in July, and they are much ventilated, and rise to a temperature, more people buy it and do it a little)

4 - locusts:
Male agricultural scientists and foodstuffs that the most serious locust species is the Desert Locust, which spreads horizontally from India to Morocco and vertically from the shores of the Mediterranean to the equator ... and often spreads in North Africa in the spring, in one message to Prince Ali bin Yusuf (500-on / 1106-1143) and describes the devastation that it creates the locust says ::
(The locust, although it was intractable, as they say - the study is published - this is a carbuncle move that the country was going to

worship alone.corruption..bottom, in a valley filled with grass and its flowers Meteor ... his coal-black wit does not find where the hyenas Arad and the vegetation of Astragalus ..) The locust raided the country of Morocco year he / 1228 the world came to harvests of all kinds the rise in prices for wheat and various food products and repeat in the coming year he / 1232 Council of Oman, because his country Morocco, the Middle East and in boots yield quotes and lack of payback of the Earth and went most of the production, affecting man and animal with the description of the son of the doctor (4) This disaster, saying :: (Bone drought hit the sports atrium save the plateau in front of the party and the objects of the Earth one haircut why the plant short face of the Earth over Iron slag like rackets pawn libs coarse aerial bombardment for the legs and our terrible sap burned out and what was the star of the early seeds and active plants continued past the leaves of the tree die which did not fall continued until the dry skin became skin ..)

5.war and law:

The form of unrest and strife is a key feature of the medieval era, as the costs of ending the war even escalate, leaving behind devastation and destruction, as well as famine. In it, the son describes the bathroom furnishings undertaken by the Marinid Abu Yakub on Tlemcen in the year that he and the tribal leaders built a house there that was hostile to the market and saw how they took a risk, where the third-party vandalism began to work Tlemcen.: (They cut the fruits and they were wells and they went out in the spring and ruined the planting project did not pretend that food for the day was far away will be from cider and Duomo, in one of the campaigns of the marinid Abu Said 'Uthman ibn Yakob (710-On), which came after a bad relationship between him and Sultan Al-Zayani by Pope Hammu Musa I (707-on) when I touch my father happy progress of the campaign in their aspects, the predominance of Abu Said in his strongholds and his subjects and other suburbs in the store that they got to refrain from introducing the thing that raised The increase in political instability within the state, see caused by the internal struggle for power between the branches of the ruling family, the inability of the state to protect its borders, prompted this list to control the government of its neighbors, Hafsids and Marinids, for example, contributed to a fierce war between my father and Moses, the Pope's second cousin. Xian Bin said in the period between 762 - he is his marinid Abdul Aziz, the probability of Tlemcen in He ..

6 - taxes:

It was the state to see taxes heavy and varied, increasing money for the creation of armies and training for the south, and the agricultural industries were most affected by the collection of cars, it was a political disaster for the peasants, where forced to pay taxes I could lose this situation, the farmers had every incentive to labor and production, where they were forced to give up their land, some also reduced the area of land that belonged to the doctor's son.: (They cut down the trees of their land and plucked the set, she entered through the marinid of Abu Al-Hasan Ali ibn Osman from Tlemcen years he raised her from the cave what was the usual despicable ..- and where the kneecap means for firewood and chickens and eggs, hay and all the other comforts that the strong and the weak lack - .. and raise also the weakening supplies in the disappearances, and bring fasting in love with water and watering the heavens amazed the patent will be communicated to the dialogue and enthusiasm, and that they were killed. Disaster and loss, and injustice of what is not under the limitation .. Forbidden for touching the Moroccan mid-incidents is almost doubled by God's favors and judgments ..)

7 - internal conflicts:
These were internal conflicts for power between the branches of the family, see the incident and the brutal war that followed between my father and Moses, the pope's second cousin. Xian Bin

said that it had a negative impact on labor productivity, in general, they left behind a war of destruction and hunger .. and led to the split of the state, see into two parts of the eastern half and includes the territory of Eastern Algeria, until the very heart of Algeria was almost ruled Xian's father, a segment west of the city of Algiers to the western border of present-day Algeria and almost falls under the authority of the son of Hammu Musa II and security conditions agreed .. Ibn Khaldun said :: (If the name of the limits of his reason either holds the airfield in the country in need, or the period the emergence and war due to the fall of kings, while this period signed corruption in the dialogue of the village and its rotten pills kept the interrupted roads and utilities for her and the peasants, when it does not become fields for several years, only a scene or just a transit corridor for detachments of warriors who rise to the region and engage in scorched earth politics, then the peasants belong to and from attention, either for themselves, or not pay attention only to the minimum that is enough for them to live - food ..)

8-epidemiology:
Morocco was a hotbed of love in the Middle East, which has all the precepts of Zayani almost, did not irritate people with the plague, but even more cruelly them .. Decryption awaits at the head every ten or fifteen years or twenty years almost lead to the loss of a large number of people studies show that the first plague to sweep the world was the plague of Justinian (5) in the seventh century, and after his return to patrol for two centuries, it suddenly disappeared in the second century AD, only to reappear in the fourth century from Central Asia, where it appeared in China in 1346 and swept Europe, and reached North Africa in 1349 of the world, and he knew the names for different of them: the greatest plague and the Black plague ... and the black ... and the Black plague. ... and a big one ... and a year in the yard .. He began to plague his first session in Morocco and the Middle East during the Marinid era of Abu Al-Hasan (he / 1352 peace), and then an

outbreak during the reign of Sultan Al-Zayani dada of the happy Osman II (he / 1353 peace) .. Then reappear during the reign of Sultan Al-Zayani dad Hammu Musa II year (he / 1389), then the year (he / 1369 peace) and (he / 1376 peace) .. it was the second wave of plague that hit the whole world and I hit Egypt and Europe, lining up to be summoned by B (Epidemic II) And then tempered the plague for a while, but reappeared in the reign of Abi al-Abbas Ahmad Sapiens Ibn Abu Hammu Musa II in the year 1442 of the world Did Ibn Khaldun's contemporaries describe him in order to spread an accurate description, saying: (Tavern urbanism East and West in the middle of this third century, the plague sweeps away surrounded by nations..so the people of the army turned and rolled many cities and erased them, which came to the state at the time when the pyramid and reaching the edges of the range and the PKs from the shadows reduced him down to his power, that for the withering and decay of the conditions of the Imran Land and the diminishing belittling of man, they sowed chaos in the rest of his life, factories and studied the ways and knowledge of the world and home, as well as houses and weak states, tribes .. seems to have descended in the same way as they descended in Morocco, but in terms of the ratio and the number of urban ones ..) And it was the spread of this plague that returned for two key reasons: A-trade relations that connect the whole of Fez and Ceuta with it and meet a person in that time with European countries throughout the Mediterranean and between them also, and the transition of trade between its spread with the epidemic everywhere is sweet .. I have confirmed some medical research that the plague was not available for the Land of Morocco, the Middle East, but came from outside, in particular through ports where ships were taken from Europe carry with them a microbe, Rus (6), either by a rodent that moves from the ship to the pier, or by wounded sailors. B. military campaigns, we conduct Abu al-Hassan Merinid and his army in Tlemcen, especially in Morocco and the Middle East in general, they were soldiers who carry an epidemic with them wherever they meet .. As for the symptoms, it is definitely possible to make her the daughter of Merzouga, saying: (This is a malignant permanent fatal fever..it is mostly longing followed and no rest at all , but his heel of fever may be followed by a spasm of software in batches and Murari vomiting with a thirsty patient and then spitting out the human brain and then screaming, and I was out behind a human ear a pimple he died and then came out to a man Big can also be fast.) The spread of this pandemic in the country of Morocco has resulted in thousands of victims .. Ibn Khaldun: (He follows the people of the Earth. house..it is to spit it out of blood and check the whole nihilistic ... died, creating a lot of one of the whole village, which became ashes.) Ibn Marzuk: (The plague came to most of the inhabitants of Tlemcen, it was even said that only ten, and it was even more deadly for children who did not reach milk and poor people of fragments, like long-term possessors and clients, it was for the treatment of Yusuf ibn Yahya, the grandson of the world, children died out in the epidemic, and also the jurist Abu Abdullah Muhammad ibn Yahya died the best scientists of his era in science psychic died as the world of Tlemsen Abu Mussa Issa famous son of the Imam and other scientists of the world Tlemsen Abu Mussa Issa famous son of the Imam and other scientists of the world of Tlemcen Abu Mussa Issa famous son of the Imam and parents too .. As the Hulk in the world of Tlemsen and Maghreb Sheikh Abu al-Abbas Ahmad ibn Abd al-Rahman palpates the famous son of Zeagu) Ibn Khaldun: (And to remove since then the science that has arisen about the dump in the collection and thirsty for the acquisition of virtues that the plague swept away the appearance of objects breasts and the Presbyter Ian, as a bulk in us from the Nations (Tlemcen), how the achievements of its flags, how they suffered from ordeals, decreased: in this Testament, the fodder markets of Morocco carried out construction and cut out the support of science and education ..)

9 - high cost:

It is only natural that war and epidemics, which led to a large number of victims, affected the economy due to the lack of farmers to cultivate the land, which led to trade ... where are the prices, says Ibn Khaldun, describing the high prices that accompanied the hungry years of he / 1293 peace and obeyed the year he / 1363: (With a pound of salt two dinars ... as well as harvests of butter, sugar, honey and meat ... some claimed that the chicken reached eight dinars of gold the price of beef per stone is the weight of gold, lamb, seven and a half whit so all the meat of mules and donkeys for the price of Whit is good for ten dinars..the statement of a salad with twenty dirhams..a cabbage five ten dirhams and a pound of jurisprudence, a photo of forty dirhams and a pound of option three eighths of a dinar and a pound of watermelon three two dirhams and figs And pears from DHS two ..) Of course, the spread of the phenomenon of looting has worsened, which took on real dimensions in the shadow of chaos and a weak central government, the lack of security and the intensification of price increases forced my mind to stay connected for a month. he said there was a lack of security in the highway and on the roads: (This is how it was in fear and the conviction that we would learn the whole coming from our arrival safely, and then we regret when they resurrected us ..)
So, the reasons are such that they lead to disasters and the groups are almost identical, despite the variability of the territory .. they are located in Baghdad, just as in Egypt and Algeria they do not deviate from class and access .. Natural factors of drought, storms and pests insects + disorders internal and external political correctness of war, splits + epidemics .. cause all this lack of experience and .. Vince for the high cost of use on the rise Power and banditry and insecurity .. it all ends on the board ... and then people from human nature and the law of the jungle, as we will see shortly .. There have been many areas, as I said, throughout the long history of Algeria - ... throughout the history of the state see ALSO..It has been several months from these places:

1 - field he / 1374 world: It so happened that during the reign of Sultan Abu Hammu Musa II, it is interesting that this advice was not limited to Tlemcen, it extended to other areas of the world, says Ibn Khaldun: (In addition, other diameters of Morocco also tormented this year (he / 1374 the world) was great, Morocco, Oman and out..in Mallorca this year was named the year of famine and only the Nordic countries did not work from this board) You can go back to the reasons for this famine that gripped Tlemcen during this period for two reasons: A. climate variability and a strong hurricane that swept the country of Morocco, the Middle East and confirms what Ibn Khaldun said: (A violent hurricane triggered devastated the clutch of Tlemcen and theirs) .. B. war fought Abu hammu Musa II during his reign and the civil strife that accompanied him played a significant role in the affected peasant says Ibn Khaldun: (this also happened as a result of catching fire with his own hands, the majority of which is located in the territory of another states from the period to a decrease and frequent withdrawal of the Kharijites in a hormonal state ..) And Ibn Khaldun said from the very beginning: High prices began, hunger and death in Iraq, and then in Egypt ... even I heard that people eat each other, then I got a touch and hunger and lacked the fact that I have the strength to make them half of the collection every day for this, and they meet in the rehabilitation center spaciously and appointed to say that God saved him justly between them. Replaced hunger with Oman with an expensive one, so I bought one of them who is Abu al-Abbas Ahmad the famous hedgehog son of a high price food casino in the city of Tlemcen by this board, as he could not afford the exorbitant cost of his daily four dinars in gold without the advantage of big hands and a big one that does not sell no food. In an attempt to alleviate the suffering of the people, Sultan Abu Hammu Musa II issued a decision to take care of the vulnerable and the needy and the poor and to attach them to another and (7) city and provide them with food in the morning and evening throughout the winter and spring, since the opening of the parish is a planting material and allowed for sale and reduced their

prices in accordance with what is offered by the famine conditions and provisions, and Abu Hammu Musa II, like other sultans, built Xi'an carefully to store water and supplies in anticipation of such conditions and others, and calls on the people To save and store supplies every year, the prevention of the Pope's predecessor's car protected Moses in the first place ..) So he spent the night .. Do you know what is the reason? ... The reason is to strengthen the people and stock up on supplies while awaiting the Council. Do you know what pushed him to this? .. This is the board that hit Tlemcen in the reign of his predecessor Abu Hammu Musa the first .. Free vile shit right now .. Here under shyness: 2 - 698-on / 1299-1306 peace: Described by historical sources, Great famine, great famine .. This happened because of the long siege imposed by Sultan Abu Yakub Yusuf, the marinids of IT .. where this began to happen here he / 1299 peace and ended in 'Dah he / 1306 whatever, which took a period of eight years and three months, this should have had a serious impact on the population of the city of Tlemcen so that the military and all its lost fortune took note of in order to see most of the cities of Morocco. The Middle East and as a result found the inhabitants of Tlemcen from hunger, not satisfied by the nation .. And starting to rob houses of the marinids, write proposals and issue their orders to kill everyone who enters Tlemcen with goods or food and the time affecting the population inside it lack of boots exhaustion stores, the rise in food prices, grain, vegetables, fruits and other objects in the marginal cost exceeded the fashionable - as I said - the water people lost their money and their savings life so that the bear population carried this area and died there from them create a lot to unscrew the deadly hunger more than mortal force. Historical sources show that this left many victims .. Where historians say that the city of Tlemcen was deserted, more than one hundred twenty-five thousand people were not inhabited, at least only five thousand inhabitants were not relieved of this rule .. What was people's reaction? ...

Ibn Khaldun said :: (... Until they ate carrion, cats, mice and insects from cockroaches and spiders croup photo..and all animals,

Scorpions and snakes, frogs, etc. to twist the winner of any of them, parallel fear runs away share the fruit of one .. and probably eat it and kill it after hyperspeeding him and his hunger and his fear, even a deficiency of the whole and then the technician has a lack of it. They rejoice and then make a gate in the sun until the earth returns, begging him easily .. Then their hunger reached that they ate the pieces of the dead and then baptized to eat some some left the dance angry they say it and then practice it like crumbling eaters on the set so that they only leave the bones of necrosis .. Users at the same time, they emphasize access to them, cash them in and even kill them from hunger ..) Says the doctor's daughter: (The frequent death of the poor and the poor around me I hear the poor screaming at the top of their voice: The door is right into my earlobe, smell it and take it, she stayed taco th until his death, Vince, hungry for his meat will fall apart they may be from his family and his wife, no need to pay, they buried the bellies of the hungry ..) Did you see what he does with hunger? Before we accuse our father of the ferocity of Moses, firstly, that the main reason for that hunger ... advised shit above his head, let's first use the facts that we read along with what was written about this power: Ibn Khaldun for this power: (Foley after his brother king and slave is auspicious and most fortunate that Faraj Allah with his face of disaster and pressure on capacity in nearby cities and flooded the people of his kingdom with the right security, the Muslim Emir Abu Hammu Musa Ben Osman headed column of the king after he watched the loss, the rebels stormed the edge of the continental outskirts and established justice, approved a resolution of the rough, rough, hard and springy Great Moderation) So, obviously, this guy was not a cancer weak or incompetent or careless, but i believe he tried to take all measures to prevent what happened, but it looks like the natural disaster caused by Get Marina was beyond the capabilities of Sultan Abu Hammu Musa, the first and greatest of his capabilities .. It seems that it says in the end .. It is the will of God ...

Tattooed heads

I think you've all heard of New Zealand, this charming country lurking in the bowels of the Pacific Ocean, but I figured some of you have enough information about this island - rather, a group of islands and its inhabitants, and its history will be your own and really, I didn't know much either until I read about him. I'm talking to you really because this is an isolated land, located at the edge of the earth, surrounded by water from its four, and the nearest large country is Australia, and that's just the description is not a fact, the distance between them is more than one thousand five hundred miles .. it looks like the inhabitants New Zealand is happy with the level of plague isolation among the nature of their country, its mild weather, so they rarely see the name of the country, imagine the headlines .. And, of course, fortunately for them, I am convinced that countries that are not shy about their name are in the news a lot , are those happy and stable of all dials, confirms the words that the people of New Zealand have always made from among the ten happiest peoples on the face of the earth.

But let's, out of envy, the old forest, so that the inhabitants of the island who smile at God are not as safe and peaceful as the "geniuses" that we created them, and let our sites be set aside for headings, which this topic requires, so that at least a little in the history of New Zealand was not bright white, but always, as certain pages had blood red.

New Zealand consists of the Island of Giants, the North Island, which includes the capital today, and the South Island to add to another group of smaller islands scattered here and there. Scientists say people arrived in New Zealand around the 12th century AD. e., those early adepts who arrived were from the Polynesian peoples who spread their influence and settled most of the Pacific islands between Australia and Hawaii, which is a colossal work, it is amazing how peoples on primitive wooden boats simply piled these spaces of the Great Water, as they moved between islands separated by thousands of miles? .. And where do they come from in this vast ocean? .. Confusing questions Indeed, but this is not the subject of our research, so let those sailors really exceptional fight the waves of the mighty ocean hard to their little ones, to those early pioneers who walked barefoot along the shores of New Zealand, who knew later in the name of the people who came here. (Māori) And enjoy the fat of the island for centuries before the arrival of the white man.

I, being from the Maori communities of a small natural layer, often concentrated near the coast, and their livelihoods depended on hunting and capturing what comes from nature, fruits and vegetables, and the Earth was virgin too generous to them, being by a miracle incomparable on the face of the Earth. like a giant bird that resembles an ostrich, but it wins with its size and wings, which I hunt, Maori before extinction in the seventeenth century.

But the Maori drunk not only in catching death, but also in catching themselves, for centuries there was a struggle between tribes for spheres of influence. This fight is often fierce for me, the jaws of the Maori never stop eating the meat of their enemies.
In 1642 the first white man came to the shores of the country, which is the Dutch apple business. The Dutch, they gave the country its current name, New Zealand, meaning New Zealand, named after the province of Zealand in the Netherlands. The first meeting of the Europeans with the Maori was not friendly, the ship dropped anchor near one of the bays on the South Island and sent a corps of its people on a boat to the mainland for fresh water, there on the shore, the Maori, taken by surprise, killed four of them, and then chased the rest to mother ship, but the Dutch thwarted the attack by quickly firing on Maori artillery boats. Because of this incident, the case began that the Gulf got its name (Assassins Cove).

Captain Cook re-discovered New Zealand in 1769 and then took in white settlers who flocked to the islands, in the beginning there was a relationship between the population and good and planned business relations of a simple list based on barter, but from the turn of the nineteenth century relations between the parties became tangled for the seizure of a house on the ground and the construction of new colonies. There was a fight and the massacre ended, the most famous of which was Boyd's massacre in 1809, when he attacked an outraged British Maori ship anchored in the port of Ones, and killed everyone on board but five people, they did it in revenge for the fact that the captain of the ship whipped the son of the leader of one of their tribes. This massacre caused horror in the hearts of the inhabitants of the house, especially with the spread of the story of the Maori devouring the flesh of the dead inhabitants of the house, the horror was so strong that the flight to New Zealand completely stopped for several years.

But the settlers returned after a few years the plans of the new list to raise the spirit of rivalry and in the fire of the ax between the Maori tribes, and they did not need to make much effort to achieve this goal, so the ax and its problems were already ingrained among the tribes, but they contributed to staking conflicting parties into deadly firearms, resulting in massacres and wars of annihilation dropping by a quarter of its indigenous population and allowing the house to seize vast tracts of land at bargain prices as a result of the leadership of the Maori tribal chiefs selling them for weapons. which they use in their internal conflicts.

Problems between Maori continued even after the country's accession to the British crown in 1840. There have been many wars as a result of the home takeover of more and more Maori land. But with the end of the nineteenth century, things began to calm down, Oman, peace in the country, especially with access to Maori, the right to full citizenship and compensation for them large and large tracts of land for them. And today, the Maori make up about 15 percent of the population of New Zealand and their parties, as well as their members of parliament.

Appointed

In the Maori communities marked by the convention, there were chiefs and trainers, and slaves, chiefs, only their family members were allowed to get a tattoo known as Moko, that is, to be in the form of lines and patterns with miraculous ripples stretched across the entire landing page, which is no coincidence , but rather the fact that each line carrying meaning and connotation means that this person is from the family of the tribal leader, and this line means that he belonged to the doe tribe, and the other tells about his exploits, courage, etc. told that his path is a struggle with personality and importance and respect that you must submit to him. These tattoos are subject to strict laws, only decent people are allowed, and it is forbidden for women to tattoo their faces, with the exception of women with a high level, such as the wife or daughter of a chief, who are allowed to have a tattoo on the lower part of the face.

Usually among the Maori it was believed that if a person dies from those trusted to the owners of tattoos, some leaders, then they cut off his head and hold it, and they had a very special way and when preparing capes for a party for a long time, they first took out the eye and the brain, then filled all the crevices of the head from the nose and mouth with ligaments and gums, then placed the head in a saucepan and brought it to a boil over a fire for several hours, and then dried it by exposing it to smoke over a burning fire, and finally placing it in the sun for several days. until it was completely dry and then painted the shark.

This method was more effective in preserving facial contours and facial features than the method used by primitive tribes in the Brazilian Amazon, known as the reduced head method, where even the face is reduced to appear like a doll's head.

Among the Maori, they need heads - dried inside wooden boxes, decorate and take them out and put them on display for special occasions and religious rituals. The named head was dried (mokomokai), which is of great importance for the members of the tribe and the family of the deceased, since they believed that these titles were not magical powers for those close to those possessed by the lords.

The Maori obeyed not only the heads of their leaders, but also the heads of their enemies. After all, every war is about collecting the heads of enemies as spoils of war, the bodies of which are often eaten. Not only those heads to whom the tattoos were entrusted, but also any other chiefs, they were dried, and then put on public display within the village and scorned by ridicule of them.

One of the European missionaries, who lived with the Maori for a long time, describes the scene of the healing and ridicule of the leader of the tribe of his opponent with his head, which was dried and placed in a similar meeting. He says that the leader of the tribe left his head and turned to him, saying:

"I wanted to run away, didn't I? But the club-stone took you! .... And after this cook you will become a haven for me! ... Where is your father? I've been preparing it for a long time .. Where is your brother? I've been eating it for a long time .. Where is your wife? ... Here she is sitting there, my wife .. Where are your children? . Here they are, they intend to bring me food as slaves ... ".

Enemy heads were not only useful for many victories and clapping for commitments, but also went a long way in their contribution to a treaty of reconciliation and peace between tribes competing for a way to return the warheads to their respective owners.

Later acquired these titles are doubly important, when you notice the severity of tenderness and passion for Europeans in Maori, they see in them a masterpiece of rare and exquisite beauty, and they were ready to buy them for a lot of money, but why do Maori need money? ... They don't need money, they need that magic wand with which the white man kills his enemies ... any weapon, and there arose one of the most disgusting types of trade, the most barbaric ... weapons against severed heads.
It was in great demand in the (slimy) market in Europe and America, and collectors talked and store managers were ready to do a lot for it. Therefore, the captains of the ships that docked in New Zealand called them badly, and did not mind exchanging their firearms.No, on the contrary, they were encouraged to do this, because all these weapons were to be used to kill Maori with each other.

But the Maori have difficulties in meeting the growing demand for smoke, the decisions on the heads of the chiefs were not easy, and whenever there were a small number of warheads, they did not meet the growing demand, and therefore need is the mother of invention, Maori have a new way to provide capes, they tattoo heads slaves and prisoners of war, and then they cut it and dry it and sell it to European people, of course, the tattoos were not real and significant, like those that the leaders did, there were random meaningless tattoos, But the Europeans were not so much worried about the meaning of the tattoo or the personality of its owner how much their interest is to get to the top of the human body, which they take home to sell it for a certain content or they know them in their homes and brag about it.

One historian wrote that the lust for heads went to such a degree of madness that Maori warriors came to prisoners of war, killing them on the ship of captains, they called the captain freedom to choose the heads of those who wanted them, and then they returned the captives to the village, they tattooed the headlines. demanded to be shredded and stuck later, and wanted to beat them to the captain. And of course this led to an increased demand for prisoners of war, the Chen tribes quickly raided villages, the other tribes only to collect capes.
In 1831, there was a sale of heads in New Zealand, and the demand for them is great, but a small number of them were sold from time to time to the university to talk about how a British officer costs rubles, which collected about 35 - 40 heads over the years in New Zealand, he later sold to the Natural History Museum in America.

Today, there are various combinations of smoke reapers spreading around the world, already visited by the Maori, to demand the return of those heads that manifested themselves in abuse and disrespect for the people and the Maori, but in fact, several heads returned to the noise, where they were passed on to some descendants of the owners reapers as the rescue of another group in the stores without showing.

Finally, if you, dear reader, visit New Zealand, so have no fear on your head.Just pull out the Maori left behind by beheadings, cannibalism, long-standing, New Zealand today is an oasis of peace, security and development.

Mothers of cannibals!

Moms masterfully kill, boil and devour the made can at the dinner table !! ..

We are now in the realm of madness, at the point of no return, where, like language and mind, from thinking and creating history, terrible facts arise from the sick imagination of people of psychopaths and savages; for they are the heroes of our theme for this day, mothers have died.

When you share with your dear readers a documentary about wild life, whether in Africa, Asia or America, you will find that different species of animals fiercely protect their young, warn limb, and seek to pave the way for them to grow up in a warm family atmosphere. these are wild animals, but the instinct of motherhood made them an example to follow, which is sometimes the best and kindest even of human beings, especially of those women we will talk about in this article, mothers who have mastered torture and eat and cook, and enjoy what they can do at the dinner table !! ... Their stories are many, but I have picked the most recent incident for you.

ate her daughter's head.
In West Bengal, a state located in the north of India, there was a woman with a small child, no more than four years old, and from place to place next to her modest home she shared laughter and talk with her. this gives the impression that there is a lot of love between the mother and her daughter. But suddenly the lonely mother of the child in a secluded place bared her teeth and, like a hungry monster, proved with a well between her legs, and then she immediately had some kind of detachment of a large piece of meat and skin from her head, a small one wriggled between her hands and her face turned blue from the severity of pain and crying.

The dysfunctional mother did not stop and did not pay attention to the crying and screams of her daughter that she almost gave up her breath, but began to eat the meat that I had just snatched from her head.

The wife of the deceased mother later told the police that when he was leaving the house, I heard my little child available to the child, traced the source of the voice to find my wife and protect my daughter on my knees and chew the flesh of her head. The husband was stunned in his place for a moment from shock, then regained his composure when he went to ask for help, without his passage you were with your daughter in her mother's belly at dinner raw.

The police investigation proved that the mother suffers from a severe addiction to drugs and drank large quantities of alcohol on the eve of the crime.

She wanted to devour her child
In South China, in particular, in the lobbies of a government hospital, and while she was a nurse doing her daily tasks, she saw an incredible sight, she saw a young woman put her jaw on the body of a small newborn, trying to greedily eat it, and almost cut it off. his hand, the nurse only tried to prevent the deceased mother from eating her child, but she could not, she pressed the mother tightly to the baby and did not let go, a possible speeding began here and took advantage of the call to interfere with the police team, where they share these available for the little one was in serious condition and was saved from death at the last moment due to his origins in the hospital and may have suffered from large cuts on his arm and was bleeding a lot.

It seems that the reason for this act of the mad mother is unknown .. and the case is under investigation.

ate his little brain
In the United States, namely in Texas, there was a lady who was psychologically suffering and ringing in pain after a quarrel and parting with her boyfriend and the father of her child a week before her birth, did not find a way to take revenge or, rather, to extinguish the glle fire just for that to catch the poor fellow and open his head and pull out the brain with a sharp instrument, not only kill him, but also eat the brain, and I tasted it with pleasure ... no ... nothing remained of him, I ate everything whole.

This terrible situation shook public opinion in the very Heart of Texas with an electric shock not to the child's father when he heard the news that the circulation of his newspapers and space stations was severely affected and he was almost losing his mind, he told the authorities that he loved her very much and had a kind heart and does not think at all that she can do such an evil, called for the maximum sanctions against her and confirmed that they deserve to die for what I did to the son of two, while the authorities confirmed that this mother is expected to be suffer a kind of schizophrenia, and expect women to suffer from this. Sentenced to death is special and that Texas supports the death penalty, unlike other states in America.

think her kids are pigs
In the Philippines, a woman killed two of her children, one year old and the other five, and then killed them, cooked and ate them. The police arrested the woman while she was sleeping in the courtyard of the house, the remains of her sons were scattered around, there was also another relic in pots, the dining rooms were set on fire. From what you told the police, she said she thinks her kids are pigs, said she eats them.

Police said the woman was mentally ill and was suffering from hallucinations, she stopped taking medication after the crime, and her husband left her alone with the children a few days before he went to town to buy her medicine.

Hunger is wrong
In Torit, South Sudan signed an accident painful and ugly and quite during a famine that devastated the region, where they saw a police officer on patrol collecting a big man, and killed everyone he received from the stage hall where the mother was sitting on the floor, and the pieces of meat scattered here and there were chips and work, these were not pieces of Zheltofiol, but only the remains of the body of a small child, where the witnesses ate almost everything that stuck to his body without the intervention of the police, who arrested her.

Confessions of Alexander Pierce: the man who ate his comrades

We are all afraid of death, even the one who spreads the fear of death, but his despair covers his fear. The fear of death makes us enjoy life to the limit, the proposal for things beyond our

perception in order to stay alive, it is the instinct of all creatures, look that Myrna's cat are in the corner to see how it would serve you danger for their fangs her .. and our conversation today is about a man who is trapped in a corner, between the lamps of his steps and the mouths of the hungry, ready to devour him, what did he do? ... And how did he survive? ... This is a story that surpasses all imagination in its cruelty .. But if you first heard this story about the inhabitants of Australia, then perhaps you, dear reader, do not know that almost a quarter of the population of Australia today humiliate their property from convicted criminals who were deported and expelled from Great Britain (England, Wales, Scotland, Ireland) between 1788 and 1868 to serve their sentence in this boat, far and away from civilization at that time.
Here we will not delve into the reasons and motives for the published sale price of 165,000 convicts (five of them women) from the British Isles to Australia over 80 years, the purpose of this article is to develop a bizarre story of a terrifying and not boring lecture on history and sociology, but since this nightmare is an entertainment site that hasn't been devoid of culture, so let me very briefly explain to you this sensitive issue in Australian and British history that you can cause plague in a modern family or meet friends ... At that time, Britain was asked the early industrial revolution, large cities are highly overpopulated and the population, as people emigrated from village to city to get jobs in factories, this turned into a tragic gay, with the exception of a rural peasant who no longer reacted to his population, grew old with poverty, appeared tension, and tomorrow the streets are dirty - the worst thing that you have those mean, one shit in their mind - and the anniversary of the unemployed became a layered bustle, and discussed robberies and crimes to such an extent that people were afraid to walk on the roads. Despite the strict laws of the British of that time, where the death penalty was applied to the most trivial crimes, such as stealing a rabbit, the executions of many did not put an end to the crime that raged everywhere like a hair, and in the case when the death penalty was too harsh and not commensurate

with the size wounds most often, therefore, seizure and transportation came as the best option to get rid of the criminals, firstly, to get rid of the surplus population, and secondly, they were on the conscience of the judges III. And America is the main gateway to the tide, but the independence of the American colonies (USA) for the British crown in 1783 became an Australian prison, obviously sending him convicted

The hero of our story was one of those convicts who led their ships to the British crown in 1819 to Australia, the dear reader considered that we are talking about a dangerous criminal, but Alexander Pierce was not such, he was a thief of Ireland, and more thieves then, his crime retreats in stealing six mates from shoes, he was punished for seven years by Hobart, which today is the capital of the island of Tasmania and major cities (the island of Tasmania is located south of Australia and not), but at that time was only a small colony for receiving organized criminals. from all over the British Empire.

The colony was supported openly, obeyed strict laws, many of the convicts improved their behavior during their stay there, some of them spent a period of their exile in the world and then returned home, but most of them refused to return and took up life as married, they and families. and these are the ancestors of a significant proportion of Australia's citizens today. There is also a convict to prevent as well as to keep in his criminal behavior in the region too, including the Hero of Our Story who was punished with sex several times for several reasons, including stealing a turkey card, and failing to follow orders, and trying to escape , and without informing the officials about his whereabouts, steals the carriage of carry-on luggage .. Because the other treatment is an entity, as they say, such convicted Percy who never stop breaking the laws, they were sent to the most terrible place and probably to the island Sary Small, which is located in the center of a small bay called Port Macquarie.

Sara Island is actually just a few miles off the west coast of Tasmania, but access by land was not possible at the time, because most parts of Tasmania were parts unknown back then, people avoided entering the depths of the lonely rainforest that separates East Tasmania, where is the colony of Hobart West, where the island of Sarah is located, the few who dared and entered to explore the forest and never returned. Thus, the only way to get to Sarah Island was through the sea, ships were orbiting Tasmania towards it, and even this route was risky, because it required crossing a serious strait called "The Gates of Hell", aptly named since it is one of the most dangerous places of the Marine Corps and the most insidious prison that the wreck of many of them who are trying to reach the destitute on the island, thus many people who were against the prison on the island died drowned in the waters of the sea before their arrival. who writes them success from the waters of the strait Rule, Put your feet on the land of the infernal island, rather play bad luck and wish there was a strait before they see hell on this earth.

It was the land of the island, covered with pine trees and giants, but its land was arable and there was no wild life to remember, so that the sea is the main source of food for the island's population of prisoners, this caused many of them to be malnourished, while others died of diarrhea and scurvy, and purchases of rye bread with fungus, which had been stored for a long time and offered to customers. The conditions of detention are also bad, the weather is rainy and cool, and in the evening, exhausted, working all day on a piece of pine, and they suggest that the floors are stone, and are punished for the slightest reason, just by looking at the situation or adapting without permission. hundreds of sessions are punishable. There was no way to escape, a free next observer for anyone trying to escape by sea while trying to escape, but there are miles of forest that no one has ever planted a person separated from the nearest colony. The prisoners begged for an idea to escape from the island called "Beyond the Impossible", for them the trail was the only salvation from the hell of the island - to kill their partner Vit, to hang you, a trail forgotten by very few inhabitants of the island of clients.

But the inability to be saved does not at all mean that someone is not their own, despair, anger pushes people sometimes to achieve the impossible.
On September 20, 1822, there were eight prisoners working in the felling of pine trees on the east side of the island, he had the reckless Kellner and they were fed up with a miserable prison life, so they decided to flee, whatever the consequences, their plan was to kill my overseer in the assault and then steal the boat and flee across the strait to China, of course for most people at the time, the geographic information was false and misleading, they thought China was neighboring Australia and not only separated by the strait or the Great River! Therefore, most of the convicts who fled Australia and Tasmania during the nineteenth century, they consider the exit to China .. But none of them was there, because in fact there are 5,000 miles between Australia and China.

The hero of our story, Alexander Pearce, was one of those eight convicts who planned an escape, they managed already at the first and easiest plan, any control over the warden and its cost, in fact, to understand why they were heavily guarded, the prison leadership was not afraid of prisoners' escape because it was impossible to tell.

But the second part of the escape plan soon failed, the mouth of the strait was most difficult to confuse the boat with a fishing shallow, as you know, the prisoners ran away in pursuit, forcing them to paint from a boat on the west coast of the island of Tasmania nearby, then went into dark forests and landed on the off-road should have swallowed people, but rarely were they seen again. And for the record, it is even today, there are several teams, intelligence scientists and nature suppliers with the latest

equipment and a lot of pantry dare to enter to explore these forests were eerie.
It was the prisoners who knew that the Hobart colony was on the other side of the island, and went to meet the company constantly to get there, but they did not know how much separates them from getting there, and day after day it seemed to them that the forest looked like endless , walked from morning to evening, in the land of an unknown rainstorm without food, there was no game, even if they found it, they could not catch it, they did not have weapons, there was only one prisoner with an ax named Robert Greenhill, he was appointed as the leader of the group with the help of another prisoner named Matthew Travers.

Fear took possession of the minds of these eight people as they moved aimlessly in the darkness of that Great maze, there was hunger - their biggest fear, hunger is the wrong one, dear reader, probably most of us are not real hunger, which, in order to go through days without food, will not only affect your body, but also your mind, make you hallucinate, make you do things that you cannot imagine, and that is what happened to these desperate people, after fifteen days of constant exhaustion, hunger, deep forest rain and cold they got to the grave: someone must be killed and eaten so that others can live.!.
Of course, it is not required that any of them be eaten by his colleagues, so they decided to vote for the best grass that covered the forest floor, they took eight ears, cut them evenly so that one was shorter than the rest, and then wiped Greenhill also in his hand and asked each of them to prick, and the Ear of Luxor is the loser who must be eaten by his colleagues. And you, dear reader, imagine the horror that befell these people, and they stretch out their trembling fingers to hear the panicles one after another, and it was not long, until the scream is terrible for someone, prisons, Alexander Dalton, he the owner of Spike Luxor, stood for a moment holding this Spike, damn it, reflecting on the horror in the eyes of his colleagues, to meditate on him like a lamb's feast in anticipation

of gold! And the poor fellow realized that this was not a joke, when, when looking into the presence of his comrades, they biasedly attack him, and jumped up in panic, and ran into the depths of the forest, trying to escape, but he did not go far, as the guys from each side noticed, they caught and they proved him that he didn't care that he was standing with a pillar, and in a matter of moments they took him out with a Greenhill with an ax, then they cut him into pieces, they put meat, and liver, and lungs into the fire ... they left nothing, didn't eat it .. just bones, hair and nails.
It was a terrible night straight, but this is also the first time since those fifteen days that the escaped prisoners, Guerrero my eye for satiety, however, the euphoria of satiety quickly evaporated and turned into a place of horror when I woke the prisoners the next morning, the first question they comes to mind: who will be next? ..

This obsession with the terrible payment of two prisoners to leave the group and try to return to the prison island of Sarah, having already successfully reached the coast, but word of their breath there due to exhaustion and hunger. This left five districts in the group alone to avoid those listening in the direction of the company, hoping to be rescued soon, using the experience of Greenhill, who was previously a sailor and has a naval battle and the arrangement of the sun and stars. But the days passed quickly, without any gates to the near end of their path, and there was a silent hunger on them from the new, so they decided to sacrifice someone else, and later this time stop at Thomas Bowden from Durham, listen to him and so the same as they did last time.

Now only four survived: Robert Greenhill and his assistant Matthew Travers, as well as the Hero of our story, Alexander Pierce and the prisoner of another named John Mather. Because Greenhill was the one who holds the ax and the group with his friend Travers, so the next victim was no longer Pierce or Mather, the choice fell on the mother, this time did not convince, but I agree that the other three kill him, caught by surprise, hacked to death with the ax of the hryvnia.

What the problem of human flesh, according to experts, is that it is rich in proteins, but it lacks carbohydrates (sugars), which are the body's main source of energy, so no matter what you have eaten human flesh soon, you hungry, you will eat again. especially when you're constantly draining your energy in the midst of a grueling journey, so it turns out that its owner, Alexander Pierce, is the next victim, and that it's only a matter of time before he Greenhill and his friend Travers kill and eat her. But something went beyond expectations - not that course of events completely, as you know, traverse to the snakebite, Greenhill insisted to be carried, they walked for five days, but at the end of the fifth day Greenhill realized that Hope was rising from his survival friend and he is dead, killed by an oath, and this time the intensity of busting them. that is, I did not use it, but they ate the meat raw.

Now only the real Percy is not left, it is more like a game of cat and mouse between them, they both wanted to eat each other and the difference, Greenhill is the clear leader, he holds an ax, but Pierce was very careful, he carried a thick stick in his hand and did not allow any domain to join the company. Gone are the days of Tetra, I understand that the two men are still far from the end of the road, and the stars are holding on to the one who kills its owner first, eats him. In the five days that have passed with the last meal, these two men already had it completely, and they all decided to deceive the other.

As the darkness darkens, it turns out that the two men who call them first will be eaten by the master, so I resisted sleep as much as possible as if they were in a competition, and you can imagine a worker, dear reader, two people exhausted and devastated completely walks up to each other, and they both try to keep their eyes open so he doesn't kill his friend. ... The victory was won in this rockabilly competition by Perrin, who was able to resist slumber, so I surrendered to Greenhill, people fell asleep in his eyes, he got up and poked with an ax from Greenhill's hands and used them on his head, killing him, and then tore his body to pieces and enjoyed eating meat alone.

The group ran to Greenhill for 42 days, only the pier, there was no more eating there, the forest ground was less rough now, but there was no sign that the flight was completed, the green jungle still stretches to the end just like it did at the beginning travels . Most likely, it is Pierce who will die alone in the darkness of the rainforest and be forgotten, but fate intervened again, a few days after the murder of Greenhill, and while Pierce walks exhausted, hungry and desperate between the trunks of giant pine trees, as found in a food warehouse Aboriginal islanders and it was their habit to hide some of their catch in the Dead Forest to slaughter it during the Dengue fever, it was the prize of cream and unexpected health said Alexander Pires Level! ...
Finally, after Pierce's flight lasted 55 days, she survived like a miracle, once again luck was his ally, as she barely got out of the forest until she came across a flock of sheep, the shepherd her old friend had to feed him and hand over to the authorities, and soon Pierce returned to his old biography, began to steal sheep from neighboring farms, with the help of his friend the shepherd, and spent less than two months until he was arrested again.

Surprisingly, Pierce confessed to the judge - who was also a priest - in all the details boring how he escaped from Sarah Island and how he killed his colleagues one by one and ate them, but the judge did not believe this story, he thought that Pierce was piercing all these things to a boil on their colleagues who fled with him, and they are still alive somewhere in the colony. Perhaps it was with the judge right in this incredible story, the sight of Pierce doesn't inspire anyone who sees him in front of a serial killer, a monster. There were the features of his innocent face and short stature, not exceeding 160 cm.

The judge decided to re-send the pier to the island of Sara, as his partner, the patron saint of lost sheep, was hanged for being a fugitive from military service.

Usually Pierce went to Sarah Island and he was on his escape from the 113th day. The prisoners there accepted him as a hero, as a person who destroyed the myth of the island of Hell and managed to escape from them.

It appears that Pierce's master was hard-wired for pleasure, so he only drove there for a few months until he escaped again, this time with a prisoner, a young man named Thomas Cox; opposite his previous trip, Pierce decided this time not to enter the woods, but to go north along the west coast of Tasmania. The plan quickly failed, as he was arrested 11 days after his escape, he was alone and searched his clothes, they found pieces of meat and human body parts, I admit Pierce that she is dating Cole, I wonder what he was carrying stock of good food, so killing and devouring Cole is not justified.
When asked about why he killed Cole the deflected one, Pierce said that when they reached the river, they had to cross it, tell him to Cox that he couldn't swim, gestured to anger Pierce because he felt coke would be an obstacle since he decided to kill him, and when they asked him about the reason with Cole Forex keeps enough food with him, he replied that he loves to eat human flesh! ...

Whether Pierce's confession was actually shocking, it is true that cannibalism was not something unique in Australia, and Tasmania, New Zealand, where the indigenous people in those distant parts did not stop eating the flesh of the bodies of their enemies, they only heard how white man eats human flesh. Worse, he sought human flesh not only because of hunger, but also because of pleasure.

The trial passed quickly and without a lawyer, and was sentenced to death by hanging until his death.

At nine o'clock in the morning on July 19, 1824, Alexander Pierce, then thirty-four years old, was executed. It is estimated that the last phrase uttered by Pierce before his execution was: "If human meat is tasty, then it tastes better than fish and pig meat" !!.

A judge's order to hand over Pierce's body to medical authorities for use in law lessons, and the top of his skull is still fluttering and shrinking in a store in Australia.
The story of Alexander Pierce has become widely known, many novels and history books have touched and made several films about her, reminding them of a documentary (remember the last Alexander Pierce) in 2008, and a horror film (security) in 2008, and a film (Van Diemen's Land) in 2009 .

Cannibal Milwaukee

We have heard and read many stories and myths about cannibals, and some of these stories have been true and have been documented in the media, and most of the tale has been sold by people through time to scare each other, which made us wonder if there is always meat eaters for humans or not ..

Cannibalism: to eat human flesh of its own kind, and the word (cannibalism) derived from the Spanish word described the tribes of "Caribbean" India, who lived west of the Andes mountains, and, of course, cannibalism known by this tribe, and maybe cannibalism was a common occurrence in the ancient past, but now it has become a little and rare .. Jeffrey Dahmer was a serial killer and one of the most famous cannibals in the eighties and nineties, let's find out more

Origin:
Jeffrey Dahmer, born May 21, 1960 Wallis Western, Wisconsin, United States of America, the boy was normal, like other boys as a child, and was very shy, but his teachers felt that he was suffering from neglect, which led to the expansion of the family who suffered and grew up in a family of four and he was the eldest son and had a sister younger than his age, he lived with his parents until his mother tried to commit suicide with an overdose of seat pills (meprobamate), then separated parents apart and married his father again after a woman ..

Upon reaching adolescence, he was lonely and isolated from others and addicted to alcohol, he was expelled from high school, which forced his father to force him into the army, where, according to one of his own soldiers, he was tortured there, and after two years of service he was fired as a result of his addiction to alcohol, and when he left the army, he did not want to meet with his father, stayed with his grandmother for 6 years, and she noticed that he was acting strange and funny; because he stole a human doll, a mannequin (a mannequin used by a number of clothing stores), and he had a life of his own. lusting for them and then for his grandmother in his house; for she is arrested on charges of public leaving, lives alone in an apartment and found work in a chocolate factory ..

His criminal career:
When Dahmer begins his criminal career, when he travels to places where gay people are either looking for young people in nightclubs or who run away from their homes, he always focuses on victims who no one cares about and does not notice their presence or disappearance alone. twists the amount of money he seduces or prepares them to buy alcohol for them or drugs versus going to

their apartment with him and, if they do, strangles them to death and then separates the skin from their bones and practices niche with them (beautiful dead) and preferably contains parts of their victims, children's orthopedic ones and, of course, after we eat their flesh and store some of them in the refrigerator.

Rose Damen's first murder was in the summer of 1978, when I was eighteen, where a young man of the same age named Steven Mark Hicks was killed.They drank alcohol together, and Stephen wanted to go to a rock concert, but Damen insisted so that Stephen would accompany him home, and he indicated that the latter agreed, and when the young man wanted adventure, she did not let Dahmer in and he hit him on the back of the head, hit him together, then sat him down on a chair and almost lost consciousness from tea, and then he strangled him to death and took off his clothes, and then a masturbation march on her body .. And the next day Dahmer cut the body; to be able to move her and bury her in his backyard, but after a few weeks came back to take out the body and he put her in a bath to melt the flesh, and that ended up crushing the victim's bones with a hammer and throwing the bone powder at forest near his house ..

In 1979 he insisted that his father join the US Army and put him there as a medic at Fort Sam Houston.And after installing him in I think one of the soldiers that he was raped by Dahmer, as he was several times tortured, and due to excessive drinking by Damen, his performance at work deteriorated, and in 1981 he accepted his performance in military service as unfit, then officially left the army ... and then left for Miami; because he didn't want to see his father, and there he started working in a sandwich shop and started renting a room in a nearby hotel, and then called his father to tell him that he was going to Ohio.

In 1982, and before losing his job, he was stopped by the police on charges of exposing an act that was unseemly for women and children, he was sentenced to a fine of $ 50 in addition to legal fees, and in 1986 he was again convicted of masturbating in front of two children in not more than eighteen years old, but he justified himself by saying that it was just urine, and since there were no witnesses, the charge for petty hooliganism was changed and he was placed under observation for a year ..

And in 1987, Dahmer and Young rented a room at the Ambassador Hotel in Los Angeles, California, and told Damen that I had intended to just play with tea and get some drugs, but the next morning the young man was found unconscious and bleeding from his mouth with a few bruises on his body, and also added that he did not mention at all what happened, which caused him to dispose of the body, so he bought a large bag and put the body inside, then took them to his home and said he could cut off the head, arms and legs, and then remove them. the bone and torso of the body before cutting the flesh into small pieces and placing it inside the plastic bags and then he wrapped the bones inside the leaves and hit it with a Hammer until it turned into small pieces, and the whole process took about two hours. and as for the head, he needs it, and after two weeks he takes the head and puts it as far away as it contains boiling water, and then adds to the industry organization (industrial detergent based on alkali) to get rid of the meat and keeps skull to use as an incentive for masturbation, but the skull crashed while trying to sell them and so get rid of it, after committing this crime, Damen increased activity in bars, homeopathy, and also began to use sleeping pills to intend his victims.

The crime that has sparked much controversy is that when trying to kill a young man of fourteen named James Doxtator, Who took him to his home and showed him a fifty dollar sum; to take the naked photo with me, and after that, before tea, I went to the house of Damen of the last sex, and then I tried to kill him, and I barely ran away from him, and the young man found Naked on the street with Damen, and he was bleeding, so she called in two cops, but Damen's cooler nerves forced the police to leave, and the lack of mastery of tea English was instrumental in allowing the integrator to re-brew tea at his home and pump and choke in the basement, and then one more time ... he cut off his head and had sex with the victim, leaving his head as a souvenir ..

After Dayman Avenue on the second and twentieth in a gay bar, he suggested the same about the building and took him to his house and then to his bedroom, strangled him with a leather belt and had sex with his body, then cut his body the next day after he killed it and threw it in the bin and kept it in his skull ..

And in 1991 the show went on for three men to escort him to his one hundred dollar home, but one in three agreed and his name was Tracy Edwards At the age of two and thirty, he took him to his bedroom and brought with a knife, and then decided to take a picture naked on the screen to please Dahmer, he did so, and then Damen went to watch TV and inspired the young man to his side, where he was told that he intends to eat his heart, of course, tea could prevent Daiman from abusing him several times while they were sitting in the living room said the young man was born and will continue to use the bathroom, but he jumped off the couch, ran to the front door, and that's how we were the only victim to escape From my hands heck, and after that he managed to escape from the stopped police car, consisting of two police officers from Milwaukee police and accused Jeffrey Dahmer who tried to kill him, so he went with the cops to raid on Dahmer in his apartment, and after they broke into his apartment, they found under his bed a staircase leading to the basement, on which it is written that Dahmer was chopping his victims, and they found grotesque portraits of some of the victims, and they were surprised also by the presence of the heads of the victims in the refrigerator, as well as some of their limbs and genitals, try Dahmer to resist the arteries, try Dahmer to resist the arteries. but soon he gave up and was with him (what I did, I had to be dead.) And it was an imminent end, so the next legendary, he was arrested on charges of child molestation and sex offenses, and charged with the murder of seventeen people between 1978 and 1991, which is later revealed to have suffered from many mental disorders and borderline personality disorder. therefore sentenced him to life imprisonment ..

His prison and his death:
In 1991, he was transferred to Columbia Prison and placed in solitary confinement, fearing for his safety, and also because he loves to associate with the rest of the prisoners, and after several years of solitary confinement was transferred to a secure cell, where he worked as a toilet cleaner for two hours. a day, and after a short time asked Daiman from the detective to give him a copy of the Bible, and then gradually devoted himself to religion and became a born again Christian. And in 1994 he was attacked by his partner on the camera, who beat him in the ring with a razor blade, in as a result, he was seriously injured. And on the morning of November 28, 1994, Dahmer was found lying on the bathroom floor and received many blows to the head, and he was still alive, he was transferred to the nearest hospital and a few hours later was pronounced dead.

Films adapted from his life:
Until his death a year ago, the film tells the story of his life in 1993, and his name was Jeffrey Dahmer: The Secret Life (Jeffrey Dahmer: The Secret Life), but after the death of his chest, other films .. 2002 released a film called Dahmer (dahmer) and in 2006 released the film The Rise of Jeffrey Dahmer (Raising Jeffrey Dahmer), and in 2015 released a series of American Horror Story: Hotel (american horror story:
hotel), which was Jeffrey Dahmer one of his characters .

Young meat rejuvenates!

Nan is two small village near the city of Jincheng in China .. the village is primitive calm and quiet, its inhabitants earn their living with simple jobs, they have no ambitious plans to improve it a little the next day, they eat what they earn with their own hands in their fields and have surpluses to the rest of their lives from clothing and other needs.

The inhabitants of this village live like a beehive, work during the day and return at their own evening hours, which is why you find that most of them do not know who lives next to them! Because they don't have much time to meet with neighbors or babysit them. When a person loses or kills, no one attaches much importance to it, especially if this person does not belong to a loved one. Poverty and fatigue continue to force them not to think too much about what is happening around them.
Even the police in this area were in deep sleep, as well as the applied nature of the inhabitants of the region, where lack of attention to caring for anything is almost a common
feature. Moreover, families are sometimes called an accident, but they do not come back to follow her communication, because they do not have time. That is why the police find the Overstock messages in dresser drawers so caked with dust, they are lazy police officers who have adopted a boring routine, and do not forget about the impact of administrative and financial corruption on those remote areas that are far from the attention of the central government of Beijing, and as they say: "if you missed the cat, play rat "! ..

This is an area of quiet, monotonous life, where everyone cares only for themselves. it was a fertile environment for the story of Zhang Yong Ming, who was born in 1956 and raised in the area.

Nervous crazy
I knew about Zhang that in his youth he was very irritable, hot-tempered and impulsive. One day I had problems between him and his cousin there was no imamat no-knife rusty was next to him quickly she tried to pack her cousin but divine providence saved the cousin from his hands at the last moment the flood of Zhang's father and uncle who drove Zhang out of houses .

Zhang has become freer now, overshadowed by the tendencies of his criminal activities, he has become like a man who goes into the forest to say and feel his victims in front of passers-by, and no one can stop him because he knows a good place that is inhabited. But one day in 1979, Zhang was caught red-handed after someone reported that the body of a teenager lay between his hands and cut her joints, and he was about to move her away from the place where he cut her, but in the meantime he was arrested by the police that she does not want to talk and wants to share and does not want to open any case, so as not to draw attention to the corruption that gnaws at the region and puts it under the microscope.

The pledge was Zhang's prison, sentenced to death, but soon after that, forgetting about the villagers, or rather the address of the incident, the evidence in the case of his crime was changed to turn the death sentence into life imprisonment. In 1997. Surprised, the villagers released Zhang and gave him a piece of land and a sum of money to be a good citizen and cooperate with the community.

Zhang bought a house on a corner in a village and began to cultivate his land to decipher from field to house and from house to field and got it once and for all with someone, but sometimes he knew that some dried meat was sold at the food center available at the same village where he lives, and he told his clients that the meat is poultry, ostrich.

Of course, the inhabitants of the country are poor, why did they leave it for a day and they no longer know what an ostrich is, but they are the ones who buy this meat, because its price is appropriate, they were happy to have it in their village and availability almost constantly, and, thanks of course to Zhang, who only God knows where this meat comes from.
New York University and the disappearance of students

During this period, significant changes took place in China, those changes that turned it from the country of the idle and lazy to the country of the Mardi industry of Mali throughout the world. Among these changes are the construction of numerous schools and universities, and some schools and universities are being built next to a small village where Zhang hauls off students who come from far away to attend these universities, since it is the villagers who send their children to these schools new.

With the increase in the number of schools and the number of students, there was a period between the period and other company reports of the disappearance of one of the students, with all the disappeared in their teens and adolescents, between 16 and 22 years. But the police, of course, did not want to work and did not pay attention to the village began to put excuses and the disappearance of students on this matter of flight from poverty and lack of livelihood, even threatened the families of the victims sometimes in order to close the topic, this was already a reason for gossip.

The auction is sick!
On the same day in 2011, a young teenager walks past Zhang Yong Ming's house and scares the young man from behind and tries to strangle him with a leather belt, Zhang tightens the belt tightly with both hands, but openly charms the farmers into consoling them to come running to him to watch Zhang try to drag him tea to your home. After Zhang saw villagers gather around his iPad to press him, claiming he was joking, the young man went his own way.

The villagers immediately went to report to the police to be arrested in this case. But only a few hours passed, as he was released, and the district officer said: "I was joking with the guy, and you, the villagers, hurried to judge you." !! ... Why people from the village, what they say, returned to their homes.

After this incident, the same guy who was strangled finally disappeared? And nobody knows about it. Xi.

The line of disappearances continues and the ostrich market is inundated! ... the parents of the poor move on, hoping for their children to get back, while the national security company lies ominously shielding the village sky.

But for every story of this end of the world. The criminal's story, we animal people, had to come to an end.

The news arrives in Beijing
On April 25, 2012, a teenager, Han Yao and aged 19, went missing and studied business management at Yunnan University, located ominously near this village. The disappearance of this student happened in the presence of witnesses, he was involved the previous night with his friends to say goodbye to them at the fork in the road back to his house in the hope of meeting them the next day. But this poor fellow disappeared from the whole village, as if the earth simply opened up and swallowed him, they did not find any traces, he was not justified by the police, he escaped poverty, drugged his family, because his family can afford it and surpasses him in teaching , said goodbye to my friends, hoping to meet them the next day, the family is not like the rest of the kidnappers and the threat of cops will never be stopped, and I began to extensively research the sparkling pens of the press, after their son disappeared for 15 days, several news appeared in the local newspaper. that the company fell into a deep sleep and don't lift a finger against looking for their son.
It was such news, as if a bomb fell on the people of the village who lost their children many years ago, and they are suffering from the pain of the photographs, they also broke, and they went to the press for stories of their children disappearing.

There were stories of his bloody forehead and an incredible decade.

Among these stories, an old 12-year-old child was with his parents in the field helping them in the harvest, usually collected during lunchtime with my grandmother's house, and he walked right in front of her in the cornfield and only moments to disappear, the child suddenly and they did not find no trace, his parents are poor they think there is a magic hidden son right in front of them.

There is another child who was with his father found him in the field and also suddenly disappeared they think that he went to the bathroom, but his absence was never.

And another child was coming home from school, and the last one was walking down the street, and another, and another ...

Many stories have been like butter press and loud and shockingly safe years in Beijing and this village.

The Ministry of Public Security in Beijing sent a team to investigate. After the investigation team arrived in Nanjing, they found the residents of the poor region in a state of panic, and residents began to flock to the investigation team with the story of the disappearance of their children and recall the stories from the past that came to Zhang's past.

The team of investigators is also surprised how these disappearances all got lost under the cover of secrecy, with this challenge years ago. And the discovery of the investigation of the model and the secret, some information was released to the press on May 23, 2012, it was announced that the head of the company in Jincheng with the chief of police and 12 police officers were fired because they do not do any investigation into the missing number with an apparent frequent presence communication.

Investigative actions continue
Continuing to comb the area for two weeks in front of the investigators of Beijing life, the villagers intend to frame Zhang Yong Ming's house with a yellow ribbon, do not even let people out of there, and for several days the investigators have entered his house and come out of the bags so many that cannot be counted. The parents were even more frightened by the fact that these bags did not mark the disappearance of their children and there were many things that they saw inside the bones ???
The press followed some news and newspapers that the Chinese company feared that the cannibal killer ate and sold the meat of 20 missing people, and that a massacre was discovered at his home in Yunnan County. Then health became more concrete, he said that the recent arrest of a 56-year-old man named Zhang Yong Ming and the disappearance of at least seven people have gone missing recently. The police found eyes in a frying pan in his house and put alcohol liquid in bottles, they found chopped meat, salted and hung it all over the house to dry, believing that it was human, and also found piles of human bones, it looks like he was feeding his dogs from the remains human bodies.

Media reported that 20 people from the network disappeared just a few kilometers from the suspect's home, and documents were also found back to Han Yu, at Zhang's home.
What the Chinese company that looted the country revealed was that the disappearances were not cases of kidnapping of ordinary people, but that was exactly what was behind a horrible serial killer who ate meat from people. At the same time, the Chinese government has tried in various ways to deliver judges without even terrorizing the region's residents, including the region's reputation for tourists and university students. The day after the publication of the Health News, the Ripper ordered the Chinese government to immediately remove all messages and news related to the case from the Internet. But four days later, because of the

consequences of this case, China decided to break the silence by publishing the official Xinhua information about this case in the Chinese news agency with the following content: (a group of investigators from Beijing left to investigate the disappearance of teenagers in the Yunnan area, were arrested and accused Zhang Yong-Ming of Nan Village, where a large amount of additive material was found in his home and DNA comparisons of the victims were carried out, the accused were linked to the murder of one of the ten victims. Finding that the accused uses several methods of covering up his crimes, he decides dismember their victims and pay, and burn what is left to destroy the evidence). Cannibalism is a sensitive topic in China, there are habits and beliefs expressed in China, and these were their ancestors during the days of the Council of Cannibals, or now it has become a taboo so that this issue does not get into the media, is censored.

Zhang Yong Min was mute, did not move, did not recognize and did not think about anything, but all the clues and clues to his past Black testified to this. As I mentioned earlier, this was not a precedent for killing people and their interests in 1979, but he apparently changed his style and became more secretive than his former one and hiding the consequences of his crimes. Lawyers do not change much over the years, he is like a wolf chasing victims who leave their unfortunate in a traffic jam near the house, he uses his belt to strangle them to keep his breath. then inside their house they mutilate and the meat is separated from the bone and create a pot with their eyes to find them in bottles full of alcohol, bones, put them in bags and inject them into their backyard and eat some of the meat and give their word that connects they are also from this meat, he has three dogs, and the rest of the meat speaks later and hangs on a rope to dry like dried fish, and then sells it at the local market in the region, describing it as meat (ostrich). Maybe some parts of the useful edible gas will burn it along with some things of the victims.

Chinese goods rejected a permit where he sold meat for fear of spreading more panic than the population had.

Cannibalism trial
On July 28, 2012, I started a serial killer trial, Zhang refused to admit his crimes and refused to apologize to the families of the victims, there seemed to be no regret or remorse for what he did. His lawyer claimed that he suffered from a mental disorder, but the court found him sane and sentenced to death, and also found guilty of the murder of 11 of his victims, who were so through DNA.

The police and the court did not answer the questions raised about the motives for the murder.

Medicine cannibals and vampires

Medical Medieval Recipes Include Wonderful Weird

Europe lived in complete ignorance and spread it to get rid of the Dark Ages until the end of the Renaissance, during that period there was a passage in the worst stages where no one can distinguish medicine from quackery, he described the treatment when the doctor is the same as when the magician and Juggler with different appearance and method of persuading the patient and was used by the rich and the poor and the citizen of the hard worker and the prince, and the first price they are the philosophers of Greece, and I thought that the disease arises from a loss of balance, volume and that the patient must source some of his body breathe from the same user, but from the body of an animal, and that is why they thought that the development of the genitals of animals to increase fertility and strength.These theories migrated from Greece to the Roman civilization, which was the bloodiest of these. Colosseum Where was the scene of most of the battles of the Greco-Roman struggle between gladiators, its square with the blood of those who raised the plague, with blood that was about to lick the epileptics

Did they believe that drinking the warm blood flowing from the wounds of gladiators helps in healing the conflict, and it was epilepsy? People flock in large numbers for these hours to drink the blood of gladiators of the defeated two and they are in agony, or maybe they break these gladiators defeated in order to drink blood from their wounds, bloody games, and among the doctors of the Romans who suggested this, there is the Roman physician Scribonius Largus, who was a physician to the Roman emperor Claudius, and between the description of his strange that he meets a sick conflict liver fighters, and these patients had a conflict that they bring the parties to the theater, and when he falls down as gladiators, they even draws His last breath, they save, it is the bears that abruptly stop his liver and eat it raw.

This situation continued until this bloody sport was prevented in 400 AD, after the monks on those bloody practices, while the habit of drinking blood spread in Europe as a cure for pathogens and renewal, health and youth as the Italian philosopher Marsilio ficino announced to the world, who argued that drinking the blood of young people with good health renewal the network has the Senate and make their health better.

When Giovanni Battista Shep fell ill and is Pope Innocent III, it is said that his doctors forced him to drink the blood of three children by the age of ten, and later died of these children, but the Pope did not recover and died on July 25, 1492 around the world.

Despite the scarcity of fresh and warm blood, other ways were found from patients to get them in the States and Scandinavia, Germany and England, and one of these methods is the death penalty area, where criminals and traitors are executed, spectators gather there for the sight of death and match heads, and epilepsy patients also gather, and they hold cups in their hands, maybe they collect blood flying from the execution platform.

And in the 17th century, a case was recorded when one of the patients, worried about death on the platform and drinking blood from the neck of a man of bad games, not only drank the blood of criminals, but also expanded it to include drinking the blood of princes and kings, on January 30, 1649 years was supposed to lead the King of England Charles I to the death square and was beheaded on charges of treason, and the people collected his brain with their own hands, since they believed that the Blood of kings heals diseases and the same disease as the Evil Queen, and asked that the name on it was written. the swollen lymph nodes around as a result of tuberculosis, as well as the parts of the king's hair and brain that had benefited the executioner and made a fortune by selling him, dried up on the ground that day.

Recipes that were mixed and contained human remains, they have too many and the most famous description of drops from the file, or as it is also called (goddard drops) And return the original in the name of her to the world of British chemist Jonathan Goddard, at first I did not become famous for this recipe, but he became famous when he was bought by Prince Charles III, and this is the son of the English king Charles I, from Jonathan Goddard against £ 6,000, and Charles II created laboratories and factories for the production of this recipe in large quantities to cover the great demand for them, he shot at her with an elixir of file drops regarding the captured King Charles, and small bottles were sold as a sign of his neuron and dendrites. listen Demand for about 200 years and although it had no medicinal properties and caused the death of many people, and Charles II himself can try it when he fell ill and on his deathbed, February 6, 1685 peace, but he did not recover and died after this as a result of illness, and because of frequent deaths, say, the turnout for this recipe, and the compositions became not a secret recipe, but this was the middle of cookbooks in 1823, in equestrian access there is approximately an equal number of centuries, deer and snakes, dried and ivory, and five measures of human skulls, where people used this time for people who die violently, it is the retention of part of their life in their bodies and in particular the Skull, and this depends on the fact that the powder of the skulls is an essential component of access, where it is brought to the skulls of thieves' graves that were supposed to be Irish, of course, access has no medical benefit and may have gained its popularity thanks to the ammonia that is formed during the br revives such material and turns him into an alcoholic, and this is what gives an improvement in well-being and the disappearance of symptoms in patients.

And since the prevailing belief at that time that part of the soul was imprisoned in the body of the dead, or people who die a terrible death, the British physician John Frink (John french) described the strange and amazing year 1651, when he grabbed the brains of dead soldiers up their bodies in the military hospital in which they worked, mixed them with horse waste and let them roam for six months, and then sold them to patients as a medicine for many pathogenic diseases of that time, and continued access until the seventeenth and eighteenth, and found in books dating to the present day. world of 1730.

And during the 17th and 18th centuries, doctors collected mold and algae that grew on the skulls of soldiers killed in battle and crushed them to inhale to patients where they thought they were preventing bleeding, how to drink it to treat the menstrual cycle in women and wound healing when infected. And for months he has been describing that treatment is common, and the British philosopher Sir Francis Bacon.

In the field of cosmetology, trade with its people increased sharply in Europe, and in particular in France and England, and these were the corneas of the 17th and 18th years, where he was an executioner who drained fat from the bodies of the dead in front of clients for trust and so as not to deceive. and selling the fat of an animal, not a person, and about the months of consumption of human fat during that period of kings, she is also Queen Elizabeth I of Britain, where she painted her face with this fat - she even eased the scars left by smallpox on her face, and they say that she was very beautiful. a large amount of metallic lead was thrown off fat, which led to the accumulation of lead in her body and led to her death on March 24, 1603, as a recipe for beautifying the face and adding fat appeared in the 18th century Human and beeswax with the material turpentine is a chemical mixture with prescription drugs, like human fat, used as a treatment for certain chronic conditions such as bone and gout.

The English physician George Thompson, who became famous in the middle of the 16th century, did not have exotic recipes where drinking urine cured the plague, or maybe his recipes came out, which consisted in sweating those sentenced to death for healing hemorrhoids, before the rise of life-sentenced people gathered around them, to touch them, to wipe off the bride, who guides them out of her skin with the fear of death, believing that this bride has healing properties that are realized in the healing of many diseases.

Cannibalism was described by many doctors in the 16th century and by the most famous German physician John Schroder, one of the most disgusting recipes and the bloodiest is that it allows access to red, where it was not from the name of its share, and it is used in a dark prison and is chosen as a victim of the absence of volunteers for this painful torture and requires this recipe a young man in his prime is up to 24 years old, and his body is free from diseases and birth defects, which, in addition to the fact that his skin is white-red, he is connected with a network old tortures also play on the wheel, with the help of which they torture a person and break his bones to death, and after the completion of the murder they recognize his body in the air. At night, when the sky is clear, until it is exposed to the light of the moon, and then they cut his body into small tea slices and sprinkle them with some spices and aloe vera powder, and then moisten with wine and leave to dry under the sunlight and light of the moon to soak in themselves force them, and then smoke, and practice their aromas of aromas and anemone flowers to get rid of unpleasant odors, after which they are sold in the markets for the treatment of many diseases. Since ancient times, people have been amazed by the civilization of the pharaohs, and to their surprise it is huge, and I am most intrigued by them precisely by those mummies that have remained intact for millennia, and I think the Europeans that the pharaohs have mummies to protect the secret of immortality, and began to trade Egyptian mummies and moved to Europe in the 12th century, where it was trade that brought them from Egypt to Europe, where they were sold at exorbitant prices, where doctors mined the material law and spruce gum, which the pharaohs drew, click on the mummies so that they do not deteriorate. prevent her from moving, every now and then Europeans call her the balm of the mummy, where they think that she heals the skin, and poisoning, and broken bones, and many diseases, and later doctors suggested that the Mummy pulls a whole and bless this powder as an effective remedy treatment of chronic diseases, this situation continued until the government banned the source of the sale and smuggling of mummies, and what became difficult to secure in Europe, it went to many charlatans to put a normal body in the sun for a long time to make it look like a mummy to deceive people in Europe.

She was not an Egyptian mummy, it is only required in Europe there is another type of mummy, the most unusual and very rare, and it is difficult to buy it, because preparation takes a very long time and requires a sacrifice, someone has lost hope in life and calls it (softened) mummy with milk or mummy with honey, what is a mummy of sweets and how to make them?

Set out in this way in the book Materia Medica Chinese by a Chinese physician (li shizhen) and in 1596, and according to the description of "Li Shi Zen" himself, this recipe is very old, and the Arab legs made her (knowing this, there are no references yet to prove that the bride made this recipe), and demanded access to the sacrifice of one of those people on her own, and they were mainly elderly people who were over 70 or 80 years old, and who lost interest in life due to the weakness of their body and their inability to war, where she was isolated in a closed room, where from honey, and spend all the time in the bath, honey take a bath and drink it without having to eat or drink anything else, even become shit, they contain honey and water. After death, as a result of the concentration of sugar in the body, it is then put into the ark from a work filled with stone, it is closed tightly and the date of death is recorded above it, and after a hundred years the coffin is opened in the same way and the mummies are taken out after they have been infused with honey. which around her and turned into a sticky gelatinous mass, then cut into small pieces and store them in special containers and sell them on the market at very high prices, where doctors of the time claimed that fat from the wound site was eaten or part of the fat was eaten. to the healing of fractures of the pelvic bones and sides of serious and many incurable diseases.

Hannibal Lecter ... beloved godfather of evil

The history of mankind throughout the era contrasts with the millions of stories of killers and serial killers, some of which saved her human memory, while others fell into oblivion. But regardless of whether the story is told about a serial killer of the Middle Ages or criminals of the modern era, they all obey the same rule, a moral norm, where we share most of us, have a sense of sex, and how I am the hands of these villains from the laws of humanity, preoccupied the blessing of life.

But, as you know, each rule has an exception, and if there is a character who has succeeded in distorting our idea of the cross, and making a mistake, and creating new rules for himself, starting them and returning to it, then this is a character, Doctor "her Lecter ", who made the title of the most evil in the history of cinema. Come find out how the close audience understands the reason for perfection.

1) the birth of a person and his lecturer

Her Lecturer ... the godfather of the beloved's company
Shown in 1986, a solo film marked the role of actor Brian Cox
Featured the character "Her Lecter" for the first time in 1981 in the book "Red Dragon" by American writer "Thomas Harris", as well as an impressive novel centered around FBI agent "Will Graham" who suffers to catch a serial killer known as "the tooth fairy. ", and was just a minor character in Lecter, helping the hero solve this case.

It was Paul's traditional story of a serial killer, maniac, and cop clash, belonging to the arrest of the Tooth Fairy, and is backed up by a 1986 film The Human Hunter, which was a commercial flop and was so critically neglected.

Her Lecturer ... the godfather of the beloved's company
Actor Anthony Hopkins is a famous person in the film The Silence of the Lambs
And so the character of "his Lecter" passed, passing through valuable clients, to be sent from his ashes in the book "Harris" by the second "Silence of the Lambs", published in 1988 and this time also had a secondary role of Lecter, but his field was larger previous and deeper and moved away from the background of events to the introduction and slap of the villain in the face of the hero of the trainee variant "Clarice Starling". And this is confirmed in the film "The Silence of the Lambs", adapted from the book and released in 1991, and you can say that then I thought that I would acquire a strange obsession with Lecter, who, unlike tensions, continues to this day even receive the personal title of "Legend East ", despite the emergence of new competitors every year.

2) Who is Dr. HIS Lecter?

As we said at the very beginning, it was she who was destined to become a minor character, choose disappearance as the reason for her existence and become a successful detective "Will Graham" in the capture of his killer. unknown. That is why "Thomas Harris" did not see Lecter's story in his first book "Red Dragon", but one simple detail is enough, for example, a brief definition, allowing the reader to understand the connection between "Graham" as Lecter and the results of oil detective work in life.

This sought to interfere with his subsequent books, where he introduced with each new book more and more details about his character "Herr Lecter" and tried to answer all the questions that might arise from readers.

Today we can say that we have a story half full behind Dr. "her Lecter".

Her Lecturer ... the godfather of the beloved's company
Hannibal as a child with his younger sister Misha.
Lecter was born in 1938 in Lithuania, in the family of an aristocrat, where his father was a nobleman, bore the title of count and owned vast plots of land and mansions, and his mother came from an Italian family based in Milan, the Visconti family. The elder sister named "her" brother "Misha", having played a significant role in his later life.

At the age of eight, he left "his" and his family, fleeing the invasion of the Nazis, and moved to live in a hut in the forest, and although she fell victim to a group of German soldiers fleeing from frozen Russia in winter, who tortured and killed, Count Lecter and his wife and servants accompanied them and kept the children together.

And before the onset of cool weather and scarcity of supplies, the Nazis killed "Misha" and ate it just like "her" in flight.

Her Lecturer ... the godfather of the beloved's company
They ate his sister Misha and something hit the same
Here it is necessary to recall the existence of a copy of another story of the death of the Lecter family, which appeared in the book "Rise of Hannibal" and perfectly corresponds to the spirit of the time when he first used her "Garrison" in his previous books, it says that a group of farmers who aristocracy, attacked the palace of the family of Count Lecter and killed him, and then stabbed and ate the little daughter "Misha" in front of the eyes and ears of her brother, who managed to escape.

The survival of the KHNBR child, the massacre of his family, was not only the beginning of a new engine, you will see him throughout your age and will have a significant impact on the formation of his personality as we know it now.

After his escape, he joined the lecturer, who pretended to be the child of a poor deaf and dumb, as well as volunteers and bounty hunters by wealth and completely cut off from their surroundings, as he showed violent behavior towards children of hooligans and bad guys.

For example, at the end of the war and before "hnbr" was his third ten year, he succeeded his uncle Count "Robert Lecter" to find him and take him with him to France. Where he received his education at home, and in the interest of teaching him the various manners and arts of painting and sculpture, his wife inquired about the Japanese origins of Japanese culture and perhaps the reason for Dr. Lecter's love of cooking later.

Her Lecturer ... the godfather of the beloved's company
Young crime ... in revenge for my uncle

In 1951, he committed "his Lecter", the first of his crimes, by right of the butcher offending his uncle's wife and causing his uncle's death with a heart attack. during a fierce fight between them, the boy went from breaking him with a samurai sword and cutting his cheeks and boiling them from the sky and turned. But thanks to Mrs. Lecter's accomplice, she did not find fault with her husband's nephew, despite the fact that she was the main culprit, and therefore continued "her" young life as if nothing had happened, but passed the high school exam and entered the medical university in Paris as the youngest female student in this field in France. He started with an operation and then left her to die at the school of psychiatry and later in Baltimore in the United States and becomes one of the most famous community figures in the city thanks to the way he talks to a witch and his actions of the European aristocracy and a special master of oil fraudsters.

3) crimes, "his Lecter"

Her Lecturer ... the godfather of the beloved's company
The Return of Hannibal reveals many of the mysteries surrounding what network he created Dr. Lecter's subsequent story will surely pay for the fact that his criminal career is divided into two semesters, the first is a combination of revenge murders, the second is centered around the crimes committed by the "Chesapeake serial killer" ...
This was the beginning of "her Lecter" a serial killer who consisted of a series of crimes, revenge murder that caused the family's tragedy. In his early years at university, as they see "Thomas Harris" in his book "The Rise of Hannibal," the young doctor returned to his homeland, Britain, and murdered his family one by one in disgust. His crimes here were of the same character, similar to the one that ended with his first victim, devoid of imagination and development, and it is not surprising that she was no longer the target of his revenge, but so tore his victims and ate some of them, trying to imitate what what happened to his sister "Misha",

as if he wanted to drink from the same cup that he will tell you about.

This time a kiss on "her" was brought to justice, but his job due to the lack of incriminating evidence apart from helping public opinion about him, he saw the French in what I present to you "Lecter" in the right of his victims, who were a group war criminals and Nazi spies, the tournament was punished. Finally, he triumphantly leaves the tea city of Paris towards the United States to complete his scholarship studies.

It appears that it was Lecter who killed his family, ignited the flames of his bloodlust instead of suppressing it, and used his new status in the city of Baltimore as a prestigious psychiatrist and used all his talents to transform himself into the so-called chesapeake slasher, serial killer. monster and sadist, he carefully selects his victims and agrees to create ways to kill them and eat their organs.

Through the events of the Thomas Harris books, and especially those centered around the character of "her", we discover that Lecter may have committed at least nine murders, the signature of the serial killer Chesapeake, who did not mention the author of which only three only, the first in the right "Will Graham" worked for the FBI and second in right "Mason Pussy" and Lecter's second crime was recent and was the victim of his "Benjamin's Failed File". While the rest of it is unknown, we all know about the identities of our victims through the Doctor's Edge with Grace and Clarice.

Her Lecturer ... the godfather of the beloved's company
Most of the victims were bad people.
And, ignoring "Harris" of the rest of the victims and crimes, he made the details of these crimes from three samples of what a hero can do. Interestingly, apart from "Will Graham," all the deceased, "her Lecter's" doctors, were bad people in one way or another.

"The Mason pussy", like the fourth victim of Dr. Lecter, he was a child rapist and possessed, sexually assaulted his sister, and got him bad luck, "her," said he drugged him and skinned his face and fed him his word, and made the "pussy" eat his nose. Then he broke his neck and left him for dead. But, "Mason pussy" miraculously survived to live the rest of its life, trapped in a twisted machine development site seeking revenge.

The "Benjamin failed file" it was a Piper yought talent in the orchestra, how on Dr Lecter much he enjoyed all the tracks seen that Wandered by, he grabbed it, and took down his through, and left him in the church. While he was staying in the aftermath of the celebration, members of the orchestra saw them introduced to members of his colleague at dinner.

At this stage, "her lecturer" develops his ways in choosing his victims and getting them special and killing them and organizing the crime scene before detection, but this is done from all crimes working an autonomous case with him part of the artist, not usually, it was not only care about the success of his crimes as much as he was obsessed with making him a dramatized work of art.

4) the appearance of your Lecturer in the hands of justice

Her Lecturer ... the godfather of the beloved's company
Hannibal Lecter in prison under heavy guard.
While investigating a series of serial killer crimes, ice FBI Will Graham approached Dr. Lecter after he learned that one of the victims had been injured while serving as a surgery resident. And while the points of their eyes to "gray" on the old medical book represent the truth that the serial killer killed the previous victim, try to shade Lecter in relation to the police, but the doctor "his" Tesla calmly attacked him from the back with a scalpel, surgical and

Will Graham State LOL nearly killed us all. And so he was arrested in a serial killer case in 1975 and put oil and criminals downstream in Baltimore.

This did not prevent him, already in his prison, from committing a crime in his tenth full year after his arrest, where, claiming that he was suffering from chest pains, he reached the medical center of the market, where he managed to unfasten him from the open road made of paper clips, and attacked at his nurse, felt her eye, broke his jaw and bit out his tongue.

5) her Lecter is free again.

Her Lecturer ... the godfather of the beloved's company
Clarissa Sterling in The Silence of the Lambs
Subject Lecter, after his last murder, to make s dense, forced him into a frantic fight with the director of Shelton Prison.

The doctor was "crippled," the psychiatrist was ineffective and possibly impaired Lecter's versatility as a psychiatrist, and he wanted to use his identity in a serial killer case for the Gaines Academy. The doctor "khnbr" needs "Shelton" and reduces the will and manipulates in all possible ways. That was the registration of confrontations only for "my lecturer" before giving FBI trainees Clariss Sterling, three years after his arrest, and inviting him to help her and her boss Jack Crawford find the serial killer of "Buffalo Bill" in the kidnapping and murder young girls.

In the Crawford and Starling request, Lecter found the opportunity to own other Buffalo Bill victims the daughter of a US Senate Senate. And after several of his meetings with the trainee, Lecter's requests for a meeting, the senator personally revealed the whereabouts of his missing daughter, and was already transported to Memphis, and at Lecter's headquarters they detained and attacked his guards and took them away, after which they managed to escape, making a mask out of whose -that person.

Doctor "her Lecter" left the US after undergoing plastic surgery to hide his identity, and was his destination this time Florence in Italy, where he killed the director of the city library and took over his job before he will understand the local detective his true identity in seven years. This time it was all "Clarissa Starling" and "Mason Pussy" (the fourth victim) looking for Lecter, but the prevailing share of "vagina" managed to lure out a huge reward, and you are not very lucky to receive it after Lecter found out about him and gutted and hung.

The death of the detective "vagina" did not prevent him from catching his enemy with bait, before which he cannot resist. "Clarice Starling," and he devised a plan, after spending years in weaving, to threaten "her Lecter" with the dead he deserves. But, as usual, Lecter managed to manipulate his sister "Mason" and convince her to kill her brother with manipulative memories of the rape she suffered.

Her Lecturer ... the godfather of the beloved's company
The scene of sex-devouring career in one of the most memorable scenes in the series
Take "her Lecter" with you, this time "Clarissa Starling", and for several months Poole tried to manipulate her mind, erase her memories and her identity and convince her that she was his sister "Misha", but she resisted him attempts to turn them into his sister to become his mistress, and the duo disappears in 1993.

Throughout his virtual life, "her Lecter" killed 28 people and thought of some allusions and references in the novel "her" that Lecter is "il mostro" or a Florentine monster who committed a number of crimes in the Italian city, such as the stability of "pure Lecter" ". If that's true, then organize the death toll to 44.

6) the true character of Lecter behind her

Her Lecturer ... the godfather of the beloved's company
Hannibal is real ... Dr. Alfredo Trevino
In 2013 and celebrating the 25th anniversary of the version of his
book "The Silence of the Lambs" Dawn "Thomas Harris" was
surprised when it turned out that the character "his famous Lecter"
was adapted from surgery in Mexico named "Alfredo Balli Trevino"
and met "Harrison" in a Mexican prison when he was covering the
story of another prisoner who saved him. "Trevino" from certain
death after being shot while trying to escape from prison.

The doctor was "Alfredo Balli Trevino was convicted of the murder
of his lover, Castillo Wrangler" and was awaiting execution. The
details of the crime, as "Harris" said, this conflict between the two
soon turned into my screaming body, where "Wrangler" attacked
his lover with a screwdriver and his wound hurt badly, sparking the
insane doctor "Trevino", who managed to pump his friend with
drugs and move him to the bathroom, where he also killed the
sheep and disposed of his blood as the Butcher's contents, then
ended his crime to cut his victim's body into small pieces and put it
in plastic bags and transport one of his relatives claiming they are
wasting medical would like to get rid of them. Help him to bury her
close, but one of the workers on the farm allegedly doubts the
grave, you call the police and soon Trevino was arrested and
received a death sentence.

Her Lecturer ... the godfather of the beloved's company
Author Thomas Harris (left) said he was inspired by the identity of a
Mexican criminal
I did not hide my "Thomas Harris" telegram, and he tells the story
of his meeting with Dr. Lecter in such a way that she may be
surprised by the level of "Trevino" high class, and his culture is
understandable, saying: "he was a different kind of elegant."

Essentially, he overthrew the doctor who came to the Ripper, the traditional rapist, lunatic and bummer, and provided an alternative to the confusion and is the reason why "Harris" to the creativity of Lecter's personality and his "uniqueness."

Although he was supposed to be executed by Trevino shortly after meeting Harris, he somehow managed to escape the death sentence and was released in 2000 and then returned to medical practice and provided his services to the poor and needy that he passed away in 2009.

7) what is the secret of the legend of his Lecter?

Her Lecturer ... the godfather of the beloved's company Hannibal, the Ripper Philosopher! Since his appearance in The Silence of the Lambs, the Great One has knocked the personal "her Lecter" off the throne of the company without competition and has become an icon of timelessness.
We were used, before Lecter, to a certain type of serial killer who suffered from mental problems and seriously psychologically made them furry and scary, but with "his Lecter" there was a new type of killer, so to speak, or what was called "serial murderers of philosophers "who engage in crimes such as ancient, precious art, can report. And therefore, it is Lecter who tries every time to depict the scenes of his crimes and make them mythological and artistic afterwards, as is the case with the murder of an Italian detective, where they hang out after solving the belly, in the simulation of "Judas", as they say in the art of a religious Christian, or how his previous ones mimic the old methods.

"Pure Lecter" as the same kind of winder met in one person, without making him a terrible freak in the eyes of others, but somehow "Thomas Harris" in the carving of this page subtly and subtly turned it into a magical aura and charming at the same time.

A "pure lecturer" is an educated person and a background of socio-economic prestige, enjoys multiple talents, he is the greatest, and a veteran artist, and a doctor Experienced, and a cook, and most of all this and the fact that he uses a sharp mind and memory, a wonderful and mental ability over-analyze situations and events that made his rhythm or manipulation of his mind impossible.

But as the saying goes "all her dark side", and the darkness of "Lecter" was pitch, behind the mask of a prominent psychiatrist, lover of art and beauty, a sadistic thug made of human flesh that I ate with my beloved was taken.

Her Lecturer ... the godfather of the beloved's company
He has a tremendous ability to influence others.
Not Lecter, so long lol he could manipulate the people around him, and turning them into pawns in the area of his abilities allowed him to notice the arrest many times, and revenge on "Will Graham" by inducing a serial killer, "tooth fairy" to kill him, and perhaps his masterpiece, the greatest has been manipulated as "Clarice Starling" and eventually turning him into a feminized version of him.

But in turn, Lecter's charm lies in the selection of his victims, his purpose of murder and cannibalism was not the murder itself and not the desire of a sexual sadist, as is the case with the rest of the thugs. It is a kind of self-discharge that gave him to himself in order to rid society of its destructive elements, whether they be rapists, sadists like "Masonic pussy" or people without talent like "Benjamin's Failed File" or greedy like an Italian. In the eyes of "her lecturer", each victim was aiming at her, she was a weak link in a chain, or a rotten apple could threaten the whole world.

And therefore the moral superiority, justified by the murders of Lecter, managed to tickle the people's problems and was transformed in the imagination of a serial killer and cannibal into the "Black Knight" of the struggle for justice, but in its own way.

A successful personal "her lecturer" in breaking the case, the difference between reality and fantasy, even now in the minds of people of flesh and blood. And these were the first fantastic characters who deny the Academy of Psychiatry to study them in an attempt to decipher the island of psychic contrast, but Dr. Lecter knows when Psychiatry and his tests, I cannot doctors after I have defeated the horse of doctors and my father, but it remains a mystery beyond the solution, and sticks out of oblivion.

king

But what is this file "fried" of sin to do with it? ..

Lead the king and then they ate him !!
George's dojo office
Here is the story in short, his name is Georgia Dogg, he was born in Hungary in 1470, he spent part of his life as a soldier, a mercenary, another brave and stern Bass.

In 1514, some nobles were appointed who mobilized the army and trained it in order to lead a crusade against the Ottomans, who then expected a threat to the states and kingdoms of Eastern Europe.

Georgia mobilized 4,000 people from peasants and seminarians, the poor, the oppressed, and trained them to fight for a couple of weeks, but in the end he did not step this generation an inch from his place, the courtiers did not provide him with food and tourists, as promised, which caused outrage among the interns and ignited the spark of rebellion and revolution ... and the active ones attacked me, burned the castles of the noble and the rich and told about them, plundered their property, and soon it, and several cities fell in the hands of the Georgian rebels, many of the noble were killed, especially those who knew exploitation and cruelty.

It is said that Georgie himself was not satisfied with some of the massacres committed by his followers, but he lost control and could no longer contain them.

Thor of peasants shook the pillars of the Council, bypassing the fears of the online, as well as the nobility of the state and neighboring kingdoms, fearing that the fire of the revolution would reach them, and ordered King Vladislav II to urgently mobilize an army of tractor drivers and include a large number of mercenaries from neighboring countries to control and suppress rebels ..

Indeed, the tsarist army defeated the rebels, killing some rebels and capturing others, including Ha herself.

Lead the king and then they ate him !!
They put the iron crown of the protector on his head.
After the silence of the revolution, the nobles met and they decided to make Georgie and his friends so that no one would dare to have members of the poor of the revolution in the future, so they erected gallows in bulk, and solid ones, when thousands of people burned the huts of the peasants, and raped their women , and enslaved their children, or the most disgusting punishment was given to Georgia .. telling the nobles that he aspired to be a king, so they decided to stop him already a king, but on his way .. The way to the public square, where he was waiting for "iron throne "under fire, seated George on this bougainvillea throne, tied him with chains so that he would not move, and then an iron crown came, they put him on the fire until it turned red, and he put it on top of the GA, and brought a hot mace like fire, and he put it in his hand, and so he was crowned king! ... On the throne of fire ..

They not only did it, they brought his little brother and killed him right in front of him, and tore his body with axes and divided him into three parts, and then they brought nine leaders of his army, from those closest to him, they starved them in for several days, and then they brought the skewers of the iron protector and sewed it into the body of the Georgian, cut down by him, by his flesh, and then ordered nine people who eat the meat of the Georgian roast .. which was rejected by three or four of them, what do they do, killing them on the spot and cutting them off and rip off their skins .. as for the rest, they agreed and ate the meat by oath, all this Georges saw alive in agony and screams ..

Guide the king and then they will eat him !!
An image for dos, and his companions ate his flesh.
Finally, while the difference of Georgian life, they cut open his body and took his head and advised him on a high mast in a public square. The men who agreed to eat Georgia's flesh let them go.

In fact, these are the saddest evil killers who have heard of him personally! It is true that in the Middle Ages, and in all kingdoms and countries, there were a lot of reprehensible, ugly, terrible punishments, but this is the most terrible thing that I have read ..

The reaction of the nobles to the revolution or the state of the poor was very sharp, according to some statistics, seventy thousand were killed and tortured, it is not surprising after such a development of events and the fact that the people did not fight and did not resist when in 1524 the Ottomans came to invade the country, but Fell with ease.

Today Georgia is regarded as a national hero, a rebel against injustice, a martyr for freedom and provides a statue of the Virgin Mary at the place where she was executed, as there are streets and squares in many cities in Hungary, Romania, Serbia that bear his name.

Celebration of six napkins

Sometimes it seems to me that after all these years of reading and writing about horror, crime and ugliness I will not find anything new and, believe me or surprise me, but it always shows me something new and disappointed, and I, once again, that the crazy man has no boundaries, the new format for the day is a man, or rather a monster, his name is (James S. Jameson), a descendant of an Irish family, also a rich whiskey factory, keen on exploration travel to Africa.

In 1890, James joins a trip to the Congo led by British explorer Henry Stanley to siege the Ottoman governor Emin Pasha, who was trapped in South Sudan during the Mahdian revolution. In addition, European explorers annexed the famous Tepe (Hamad bin Muhammad al district) with the next flight to Zanzibar, who owned large farms and traded in ivory and slaves.

Of course, that era was too dark for the Congo, Africa in general, which experienced a fierce struggle for influence between the colonial powers, as a result of which the country's situation deteriorated greatly and became a dangerous place where gangsters, bandits and primitive tribes of the middle class live.

According to Lev Fran, the implications of market properties for the trip, Jameson told him that he had a great curiosity to learn more about the practice of cannibalism among the tribes of the remote jungle regions. He said he wanted to share this practice in nature and drew the details.

To do this, buy James from one of the slave traders a child of Africa ten years old, compared to six napkins !, and then take her with the local leader to a hut inhabited by a group of men, a cannibal, and ask the translator to tell them the following: "This girl is a gift from a white person, and he wants to be eaten. "

The men carried the girl to the Note and tied her to a tree, then stabbed her in the stomach and left her to bleed. The poor people began to exclude the idea that Jameson and his people would join them, but when I saw them, I did not care, and they gaily watched as the innocent child succumbed to the interests of a black man, quietly, it had already been lying for a while until she died , and what bared her breath, until her knives skinned and frightened, they put her charred flesh on the fire, and then they sat relish in the square, all this was busy drawing details of the process with an accuracy of six paintings in watercolor !.

A few months later, the news reached the disgusting pages of some European newspaper on the bus, there was a scandal for the lesser who tried to justify and justify what had happened by a letter to the New York Times, in which he said that he had received an invitation to the house of the tribal leader of the analyst and when they were present at it, the ritual of eating the flesh of people went ahead with leaps and bounds, and Thibault Tepe is the one who offered to buy the girl's side for six handkerchiefs, and that personally he would think that what was happening was just entertaining, and would think, that he would love it. to devour human flesh for real. She also accused translator Lev Fran of being angry with you over a problem that happened between them during the trip.

Of course, a lot of people did not believe in these arguments Wahu, he was not forced to buy a girl, he was not forced to stay and look, but drawing all these pictures is disgusting, but so that he was really ready to share it. As the aircraft commander, Sir Henry Stanley also saw against Jason the description of his hipster - this is a personal arrogance.

Fortunately, James did not live long after this incident, where he died in Bush due to protection a few months later. The consequences of Lev Fran were later forced to retreat from him under pressure from a British officer, Francis de Vinton, a travel destination and delegate for the peace of the Belgian colonization of the Congo, perhaps they did not like the fact that a person is stigmatized, served by this kind of barbarism.

Finally, I don't know of any minimal crazy. that's where the child is six areas to enjoy the abnormal person to see her killed and eaten! ..

The strangest serial killer in Venezuelan history

Says the district recalls: "I was alone, hungry, drinking wine, like under a bridge - the bridge allows the fast bus were Libertadores in San Cristobal, one of the largest cities in Venezuela - and this was the time when I never completely disappeared .. A young man came with muscles and a body drunk hard, sat down next to me and watched me drink wine, and then did not move ... did not know ... he started my patience, and my stomach rumbled, and I took a club-made made of bamboo - I hit him ... and beat him unconscious ... then Odette with her life with his neck with a knife flooded me with a feeling of happiness and triumph ... I've waited so long to get good food over the past few days ... after that I came with my knowledge and started to cut my body I want what I bought it ... together and a blowjob for the best soup, healthy ... heart, liver, impressive holiday barbecue for sure ... or they there is the next day ... and the rest of the text - located next to the bridge - and in the oats are gone ... you push your head between the sand !! "

In a country that hardly has a history of serial killers, claiming to have opened a "zone" of this story with the blood of these victims. Durrance File Areal is a serial killer and cannibal born in 1957 who grew up in a farming family and lives in the border zone near Colombia, most of his family members are members of a guerrilla warfare group known as the Nose of Venezuela, which controls the area the forest in which they live, and who appeared on the "area" by strange behavior at the age of fifteen, thought his family that he was possessed by "evil spirits" - this is already a touch - told his way and left ... from the main cities of Venezuela - Under The freeway overpass was the Libertadores car depots, a place too dark at night, often used by drunkards, drug addicts, beggar shelters ... he started with drugs and hard alcohol.

During the decade of the nineties, many people living near the bridge went to the police with a statement that their relatives had disappeared ... so I started drinking it quickly, quickly.
In 1995, the company began to survey the area under the bridge after the brother of one of the missing reported it, he last saw him when he drank wine and talked to the "districts" ... and was found by the police during a search operation the remains of many men in the river and among the sand, and they began to look for the "square" that lived in the bush near the bridge, inside a small hut.

One night at about two o'clock in the morning, a boy - Juan Carlos Meneses stopped by the bridge - with his girlfriend in the car, and while the change of small children, I heard something moving next to him, and when I turned around, I was surprised to find that the beggar - the square - was going to hit him in the head with a baseball bat, but luckily there was a policeman next to this place walking on his motorcycle and saw them and caught the "square" at last.

After the capture of the "zone" in 1999 and the discovery of him by a company on many of the bones buried near his hut, I admit that the "zone" killed and ate at least 10 people in the two years before his arrest, and before the trial he was examined in his arms psychologists ... they all agree that he is a psychopath in order to stop the boat in confusion, so he ordered the police to lock him in solitary confinement until now, because it is dangerous to society, and suggested by some locals that the "area" was used as a scapegoat for a gang of traffickers, and confirmed that all of them, even the assassins he hired, were afraid of him at the time.
During the first TV interview after his arrest, he told the "zone" that "human meat is delicious and I eat all kinds of meat, including beef from dogs, cats, lizards, but I used to kill bodybuilding men well, not women, because they are on the taste of meat contributes to bad, and certainly I do not eat meat of obese men who do not even beat high fat in my blood, as well as the elderly, because their bodies are infected with diseases ... "and ended with the words:" I am not ashamed of anything, they they put me in this prison for nothing. "

Karl Grossmann: The Terrible Butcher of Berlin

When he freezes, his humanity becomes dead phones and the lives of other merry, and blood - joy, the screams of victims, music .. I know that you are in the presence of a serial killer, and Atid does not know mercy at all. this description also applies well to the hero of our story, the Ripper of the German Terrible "Georg Karl Grossmann", for which he received the nickname "Berlin Butcher".

His full name is Karl Friedrich Wilhelm Grossman, who was born on December 12 to unknown parents, so he spent his childhood in an orphanage, and after he reached a working career, he finally stopped working as a butcher.

Let's remember that Karl was with someone from asocial, sadistic, excited, flattered, and maybe that's why he never married, because of his fear of having one, although he has many connections with women ..

When the First World War broke out, and the high cost crisis in the markets, and meat became expensive and not everyone can buy, and Karl had evil thoughts in search of a meat alternative .. to be cheaper .. and more! ..

It was Karl Grossman who found himself in the flesh as whores, and not a strange bitch, and here I was the first to risk a bale who had fun with them all my life, a specialist in their search, and do not forget that their number has doubled due to economic difficulties, who touched the country with war ..

So Karl began his journey through the world of murder and bloodshed ... he dragged girls and women one after another from brothels and nightclubs to rented apartments, and explained the wine with deliberate fright even to garbage, for the beast is fierce and they also go slaughtered, after which began to cut and process meat in order to sell it in the Berlin market in the morning, claiming it was pig meat.

Sometimes he made a prison web from the meat of his victims in the form of sandwiches at the station to the train near his house .. It is strange that Karl was killed not for the sake of speed, but out of his love and tenderness for his functions as a butcher, he did not come close to the property of his victim, according to the statements of the German company, it was designed and his message is written on it: (I am not a thief, I am a butcher) !!

On August 21, 1921, Karl was busy with his usual work with a new victim, when he heard the sounds of scuffles and screams coming from Karl's apartment next to the landlord, he hurried to file a report with the police.

When the police searched the apartment, there was a surprise. there was a woman who had been flayed and hung on a hook, and Karl prepared to chop to say to preserve her flesh in the morning.

Police arrested the Ripper, was finally brought to trial and sentenced to death on July 5, 1922

On the morning of the implementation of the government find, the warden of Georg Karl Grossman was found hanged in his cell, he committed suicide after amputating his hand and wrote with his own blood on the wall of the dungeon:

(I am a poor man, but I was inhabited by a horrifying serial killer, and now he came out of me and hanged me, and now he is heading through the streets of Berlin, he will happily do it again, but in a different way) ..

I wonder what he meant by this last message? !! ..

Joe Metheny: turns the meat of its victims into hamburgers!

As a rule, people are not inclined to eat sons of the same gender, but historically, especially in certain circumstances, such as folders and dialogue, people have been forced to eat human flesh, especially the dead, for their lives, as the phenomenon has spread among some primitive tribes and religious communities along reasons of faith and fairies, such as the tribe (Anasazi.) in North America and a number of India, but in our present era, most cases of the use of human flesh determine the same satisfactory (second or sadistic) motives.

As for the hero of our story, he did not kill his victims in order to eat them. but it kills them to them, like fast food to passers-by! ..

Named Joseph Roy meth, and his title The Americans and with (the Cannibal), a cannibal, and thought that the Ripper was among the most serial murderers of horror and brutality in the United States, where he did not write, killing and hacking his victims, but he said things would be worse than that much ..

Born Joseph Roy meth on March 2, 1955 in Baltimore, Maryland, to a simple family of eight, where his father worked day and night to provide for the needs of his family, except that one day a car accident led to his death. leaving it deep in the hearts of his children and his wife, who said then: "It was not easy for me especially to provide for the needs of the children, and I did everything possible to keep them ...".
It was a myth about a huge structure weighing 450 kilograms, and his family described him as "a boy, a coward, whose extra weight, apparently, did not give any of them enough time to study" !! ..
In the seventies of the twentieth century, after serving in the US Army, separated from his family, he completely relocated to internal displacement camps, where he spent the night under bridges. He was also known for hanging out with a group of displaced people in an area called "Task," and was also known as a methy in many of the bars in southern Baltimore on Washington Biscayne Boulevard, where he spent months spending his money on cocaine abuse. and heroin and alcoholic beverages, although he had a full-time job as a forklift driver where Joseph Roy was pleasant as described by his friends and also described as an intelligent, good dog and a good attitude !!

After a while, he started going to places containing abandoned houses to dump a bunch of bad friends and share empathy for forbidden items .. so you know to his wife during this period and after a short period in which she shared the partnership in turn is another addiction.

It seemed like his beginning was normal to some extent .. it seems at first glance like any objects of reckless drift with friends in the absence of any family supervision, who came that day about their life radically transformed to become a murderer enjoys killing people in horrible ways by cooking their meat and selling a burger to customers in sandwiches !!

The beginning of his criminal career

In July 1994, after the end of a work shift at his job as a trucker, usually methamphetamine would come to his house, to the surprise of his wife, he would take all his belongings and walk with his 6-year-old son, only to discover soon after that that she had run away with her lover and friends. - drug addicts, and at one of his court sessions he declared methamphetamine, saying: "I did not leave my problem to her - he means his wife, - but she took my son with her."
I lost my mind and began to spank right and left. I don't know what to do and how to produce them ...! He asks, looking for his wife and child in all places, and after trying unsuccessfully I managed to find two men, homeless, aged 33, Randall Brewer and Randy Pike, thought they were the sign of his fugitive wife, was found down one by one from the bridges, said Peter and I hunt them down like a predatory monster that moves on its prey, said Bigtits and then kills them with an iron ax, and after this was done to him, they attracted his attention by the existence of a man who was catching fish in the river is close to be seen and it is different to steal a corpse in the river. This was the beginning of his career in the criminal world.

And despite his attempts to hide the traces of the crime, but soon after that he was arrested and spent 18 months in prison, waiting to appear in court, and the trial took only one week, the case was acquitted and the case was closed, where the conclusions of the jury in court led to a lack of sufficient evidence for his conviction.

Maybe you, dear readers, that you know me enough that a lot of Crime and tease him with a thirst for revenge, but hey, so restless, I have the next physical passion of his value and zest, where he returned to his crimes again, but on this time, it seems, he had a better idea to learn from the bodies of the victims, and not throw them into the river! ..

In 1996, after the release of the prison myth, and seduced the girl of my prostitution, they were both dressed in a pub night at first named Katie Ann again (45 years old) and Kimberly Spicer (23 years old), and began dating two girls, often visiting them in Mexican restaurant, where his place of work, then began to call them in his trailer, which was committed by addiction and began to know their drug to him at once while two girls with him, tried methamphetamine to rely on them sexually, try Kimberly to resist and when I feel that resistance does not send several blows to his face, the neck and stab wounds in her back, and she immediately fell, his body was lifeless .. During this, Katie tried to escape, but could not escape from his grasp, where she caught him by the face and hit him in the neck, which led to her death on the spot ... I did not write to my met that he cut the girls' bodies and put them in plastic bags, and then sent them to his home and put them in the freezer.

It seems that the myth was in financial distress at the time! I had an idea for a demon where he bought a grill cart to quickly say this by the side of the road on the weekend and take people to buy from him where he serves delicious ham burgers or is meant for customers, but in reality it is not only human flesh. mixed with a bit of beef and pork ... and of course what kind of human meat was it for the bodies of the two girls Katie and Spice who killed them and keep their bodies in their house ..

In an interview, the myth says: "We had good sandwiches and no one could doubt or know the source, no one would know the difference between them and ham." You have complete freedom, dear readers, to use your imagination and feel the taste of this hamburger ..

And when I was near the stock of meat and two girls got to the force, he would have to go back to the hunt and try to lure the prey again in order to kill it and cook its body, and present it in sandwiches, hamburgers .. it looks like the idea liked it and began to bring funds!

This time she was victimized by a woman named Rita Kimber, where is the step to pin him on the grounds that they will be the main drug there !! He tried to pick them up and held out his hand and asked her to have sex, and when she refused to whine that of course she would not let her go, he attacked them, trying to strangle her with both hands, saying: "I will kill you and bury you in the forest with other girls . ". I tried Kemper, to break out of the trailer in desperate attempts to escape from the clutches of this terrible monster, but he chased her, hit her and dragged her to the back of the trailer, and then tried to rape her and for him in court: "he began to rip off her clothes and hitting them with a laugh available to him, a scream, but with its roundness for a split second, I managed to escape through the trailer window, "Kimber ran to the nearest police station in the area so she could put an end to Kimber's crimes. methamphetamine is terrible.

Finally, Joseph Met is in the grip of justice.
Was arrested in 1996 and later convicted of killing all Kimberly Spicers, Tony Lynn and Katie Ann again .. he allegedly also killed three prostitutes on his way to Washington Street in Baltimore, however, there was not enough evidence for these crimes other than his confession, in which he was convicted.

He threw the body into the river, but after investigation and investigation was not found by the police. And told The Baltimore Sun in 1997 that it was unclear how accurate his claims were about the number of people who were killed, although he said he killed 10 people in the Baltimore area, his lawyer said, he regretted what he had done, and that drugs and alcohol changed his personality and made him violent !!
Was tried in 1997 in the Kemper case, was sentenced to 50 years for kidnapping and the problem of sexual assault, since he was

acquitted of trying to kill her, or in 1998 and sentenced to death for the murder of Spice and again.
In 2000, the death penalty was abolished, and his sentence was reduced to life imprisonment.

I was found dead in my prison cell at the Western Reform Institute in Cumberland, Maryland on August 5, 2017 at the age of 62.

In closing, dear readers, I hope to think twice about the next time you hit the road and run into a fast food cart .. who knows ... you might end up in front of a butcher bringing you a sandwich humanly and you don't know , and remember this story well before you take the first bite of this sandwich.

A month without sleep

Around 1 am, restless headache around my head, erosion of my brain, I had insomnia and I am the ghost of the evening, so I am able to do something useful, and am able to, before the ghost of the evening forgets the kitchen, away from me, staring the ceiling of my room is boring ... and suddenly a question arose: what if you won't sleep for a whole month? ...

Meeting me in surprise, taking my imagination, I closed my eyes for a moment and floated in the sky of my fantasies, but my curiosity did not like it, and the love for my research made me get up and rush to my office, open my computer and fill it, then headed to library, where he began to leaf through his books and scientific, but to no avail? Having not received a definite answer, I returned to my computer and began leafing through the sites of foreign scientific and living Russian impressions and reading fascinatingly ...

In 1940, during the First World War, a number of Russian researchers are worried about their goal to find out the extent of the effect of lack of sleep on soldiers in war conditions is expected to happen, so the researchers brought five prisoners sentenced to life imprisonment, and they asked them stay awake for the whole month against the release of them and release them, the fallen prisoners to the document of acceptance, is it really worth the risk? Either live or die trying ...
Get in the prisoners 'room an isolated laughter channel of oxygen with a "no" gas that helps prisoners stay on their feet without batting an eye, the room was filled with supplies sufficient for months, with a bookcase and window pane to facilitate prisoners' actions, and four microphones in every corner of the room, in addition to the bathroom. in the far left corner of the room, there are all the necessary conditions for life so that the prisoners remain only sticky, for freedom ..

The days passed as usual, but on the ninth day, the behavior of the prisoners began to change, and he clicked one of them, ordered to shout loudly, then began to run around the room, to the north and to the left, then he fell down and began to take pictures of Satan spanking, strange thing that the rest of the prisoners never gave a damn about him ...

After the tenth day, they transferred the infection to the rest of the prisoners, said that they would tear the papers, smeared it with saliva over the world and poop, and then also on the window glass, and kept their sight completely, and then cut out their voices, Oman, suspiciously silent throughout the room ......

After 24 hours, the injured researchers were worried that there was no sound signal from the room, although the gas device indicated that the prisoners were alive, one of the researchers decided to risk his cross-hardware voice to say:

- Gentlemen, we will enter the room to examine you, move away from the door and lie down on the ground and do not move, otherwise we are their people, please calm down.

Getting Dietrichson's cigarette case sounds more like a whisper from one of the prisoners:

- We do not want to empty the platform and check, we are now living dead, eaters of human flesh ...

The wounded researchers around became worried, everyone fled to their homes, while the geek who remained the researcher ended the madness, he began to call the prisoners with a microphone, but Lara? They decided to cut out the gas pump for the room, and if this is done, the voices of the prisoners and the correspondence of the madmen will come, asking to pump the gas again, forcing the seeker to join the laboratory security, and by the middle of the night, having entered the room with them, they found something that they did not expect ?

The chills of his body and obsession in the same Khiva, the room was free of blood, the smell of vile nausea, the insides floated in the mud of coagulated blood, and the most shocking thing was that the prisoners did not eat any food in the room, but ate themselves, with a stuck stomach, so that their bodies tore at each side, so that the bones of their words protruded.

All the prisoners died, except for one, who thrust his jaw into the muscles of the forearm, and then began to scream hysterically and laugh terribly, drops of blood dripped from his jaws abundantly, unless a security researcher on the basis of morphine could then take him to the operating room, where the prisoner was supposed to be as if he wanted to tell the researcher something?

Bring the researchers a pen and paper, throw away the prison quill, the base of the hand is stained with coagulated blood, write: "cut off my limbs, and make me savor, and this pleasure is even greater ...."

Scientists came into conflict, saying: Why are you doing this yourself, tell me, tell me ...

The movement of the prisoner's head, and then the voice gazing at the researcher, interrupted his development, with a wheeze and difficulty in pronunciation echoed:

- So stay awake so as not to fall asleep ...

After reading this experience of horrific tricks that took me several hours of research, I got this crazy idea even more, so if we make the gas more powerful than none, then Allah is in every part of the world, will we see the emergence of the era of the living dead ? Or rather a zombie to ...?

Monster Alvendigo between truth and fiction

The window is a Kiev Fairy Tale in the heritage of the myths of American Indians in the Great Lakes region in the USA, Canada, and legends tell about the mysterious Kiev groping bodies of people and motivate them to turn into monsters eager to devour human flesh! ..

It was first mentioned in a boreal forest on the Atlantic coast when it was seen by several hunters and described as terrifying. They said that this evil spirit leads with the acquisition of a person, then they manipulate his mind and destroy him, and all the stories that were told me about this object were very scary, they spread his biography for the year of hunters, prompting some of them not to go to these absolute forests because of their sense of fear.

It is strange that the legends of the American Indian tribes are similar to some inherited Arab-Islamic ideas about sex and their bodies of people, manipulating their consciousness, especially in remote and abandoned forests.

It was the Indians who won the disappearance of the hunters of this monster, they thought that if he disappeared, one of the hunters, it means that the detachment was acquired and destroyed, and many people were not sure about the existence of this object and that this was not a myth.

The first mention of this object by Europeans was in the 16th century, when some French missionaries wrote their observations about the life and runes of the aborigines (Indians of red color) while visiting a tribe along Guam, oddly enough in the subject to those missionaries who decided to stir them up completely and did not know their fate for years, so he sent a new set of missionaries, with secret guard soldiers, to the same area to look for the sixth group, and the mission of the new look in the deep forest remained to find them, in the words of one of the group members: "They really, when they got to the forest, they found their friends, but they were turned to other people, so terrible, they are sick with insanity and fear, and hunger, some dangerous diseases that affect their fantasies and make their suffering from hunger do not belong some kind of hunger, but a hunger for human flesh, so they hunt anyone who passes by them, they said they were attacking the soldiers who were with us and tried to meet us and so he must stop them and kill them for putting an end to their madness and their madness.

This is the first interview of a white man with a window and was recorded in the book (The jesuit relations) and the Indian tribes insist that these missionaries refer to the window entities available and Wendigo in the language of these tribes means (the Devourer's company).

Look at the natives, I unwind their human beings, or how to turn them over, there are two novels, the first says that one of the ancient tribes was in a fierce war with another tribe, was on the verge of defeat, which came from one of the brave warriors and decided to sacrifice himself and deal with the devil in order to miss his tribe, and already turned the defeat of his tribe to an overwhelming victory, but that he lost his soul to the devil, and his body had evil spirits, so I decided his tribe to get rid of them after this was the reason for their victory in the war, and they drove him into the wilderness, where he became a lonely outcast.

A monstrous window between truth and fiction.
They drove him out of nowhere and prevented him from being a lonely exile.
The second novel: it was during the Civil War between some American tribes that old warriors lived in military units in the desert, as a result of some conditions, at the next click of food for three days, these warriors became severely hungry, and there was already patience for their hunger with the exception of one warrior had the audacity to do something more insane, arousing horror, in one night, while the Sleeping Beauty, alone with one of her comrades, left him and told him to kill him and devour him with the greatest cruelty, it seems that the zest serving his superhuman abilities, such as super speed and the ability to read minds and instantly heal wounds and ailments.

In order to continue the original inhabitants of this khaki object, we used black magic, because they do not curse the eternal, this shit is not a lot of things and since the stories and novels are different, firstly, this is the shape of the window, I said earlier that his form before the transformation was normal human, but after that change his shape completely, for clarity, there are not many things in the legends of the ancients, for example, there are tribes who call his creature too skinny and his body is made of snow and heals yellow tusks protruding and large, its size increases with each person says it can reach length to length of the headlight material.

A monstrous window between truth and fiction.
The skilled hunter manipulates his prey Another part of the curse is the inability to be satiated, and this explains their constant hunger and how to avoid them in trying to hunt people in every possible way, and their hunger forever is what makes them hunt people more and to devour them wild, due to their constant hunger, their appearance will always be associated with periods of long winter, and because of this, the tribes ritually protect them from window objects with some religious rites every year and dance around the fire.
For the fishermen, they described the apparatus as a tree-tall creature, thin and sharp teeth and claws, long glowing eyes, and its long tongue and body covered with hair and less traumatized by kilometers, as it smells very much like the smell of a corpse. As for the disarmament of its subsonic unit, they said so (after all, the window is an experienced hunter, but the hunter does not believe in the night).

The window to the truth does not live in a fairy tale. only there are hundreds of posts in which an American company describes a vision of this object, when parks and parks are isolated.The last call of the reportage about this monster ended honestly, linking and linking what suddenly, while searching for them, they found brutally murdered in the forest, contributed to this fact and stirred up a state of horror among the population, the more memorable incident show again a new incident, the ugliest of which preceded it, confirms to people that this object is marked along it already exists and is not just a myth.

It is believed by the original inhabitants of America that the window changed to the one lost in the forest and he lives in the dark forests of the LED that there is no life form and he avoids the light kills the period of the day in caves or abandoned mines as they know about every part of the house in which you live and has the supernatural ability to change the weather with powerful black magic, which is mostly influenced, and he also says to suspend chunks of meat on things, or to say that he is saving by using his sharp claws to keep it in if you haven't seen the victims for a long time.

According to the population, the window has the ability to manipulate human trafficking and affect their consciousness, the victim often in a single case in the forest begins to hear the voices of his relatives and his friends in order to sleep further, therefore he looks for them, like the Charmed Ones, until a certain moment in the forest, waiting windows and hears from anyone after that. It is similar to the legend of golf and Arab, which turns into bodies, and differs, sometimes in the portrayal of a beautiful woman, to hide this fact, the victim is lured, and her victims usually travel wandering in the deserts alone.

Some of the victims who managed to escape from the window said they could manipulate the weather with great ease and turn the victim into nightmares, and he has the ability to obscure this fact with his victim through burning and legend (to kill a window, you need to burn it with fire or penetrate into his heart with silver alone, because his body has the ability to absorb all metals except silver).

A monstrous window between truth and fiction.
Swift ran, surrounded by snow, with his wife and children.
One of the questions that were set in the courts for folding back to
the early twentieth century, where it was the trial of an old man
named (Jack Fedor) reaches the age of 87 and was charged with the
murder of a woman. During the trial, the man's motive for the
same beforehand strange justification of his crime, where he said
that he killed his victims because they are Wendigo, began in the
narrative of the story, he said that evil spirits came to him and
turned him into Wendigo decided to intervene and kill her to save
people from evil, and said that this was not the first victim and he
killed 13 other Wendigos, and was sentenced to life in prison and
died in prison.

The famous incident of these health objects concerns a hunter
named Swift's ranch surrounded by snow with his wife and children
in 1878 The feature is strongly expressed to say that Swift killed his
wife and child five times plays them and grows up from the dead,
arrested later, both you and the world, according to the
newspapers of the time, the reason for Swift's crime is that the
Wendigo objects took his body and buried it, committing his
nefarious.

The mysterious Tim McLean case

Is Tim McLean's problem the strangest heinous crime in Canada and the most mysterious of which is still the talk of the hour.

Who is Tim McLean?

This is Timothy Richard McLean, a young Canadian born in October 1985 in Columbia and raised in (Winnipeg) Canada, was a good young man loved by all his friends and acquaintances, and once invited his girlfriend Tiffany to work in the carnival that wanders to all points of Canada, and approved Tim for this, because he loves to travel after him on the idea that he visits all the cities of Canada, work has already happened at the carnival and helped every place in Canada and interesting experiences and new people from all over the world.

The question of the mysterious Tim McLean
Timothy Richard McLean Hear him on this course that Tim once decided that he would be your job at the carnival because he was tired of frequent ocean travel, continues to seek permanent work and returns to his country and his home.
On July 30, 2008, Tim outfitted his things and went with the carnival on a final ride, stopping in a city (Edmonton), which was far from his

home in (Winnipeg) with a very large space, he had two options: either to fly out and return home in a matter of minutes, or take a bus that takes 24 hours, and since he did not have enough money to book a plane, he did not have only the second option before him, having already ordered a ticket to the Greyhound 1170 bus and waiting for the transfer date at the second ten in the evening and the last seats in the bus ... the door opened ...

It was the edge of the road to rest because of the length of the distance, so an opportunity for those who want to spend it or for those who want to buy food or drink.

Hearing the door on your way for 17 hours, stop at the station (Ericsson) five minutes later the next evening, and entering the door of the passenger of new features, a tall Pan-Asian of about forty will appear, who turns out to be a skinhead in dark glasses, although the time was evening and later his name was Vince Lee.

Who is Phineas me?

Tim McLean's Mysterious Issue
Vincent and Shenyang to me This is Vincent and Shenyang I am also known by the name Will Piquet, was born in Dandong, raised in China on April 30, 1968, he received his bachelor of computer science in 1992 from Wuhan Institute of Technology, worked as a computer engineer in Beijing from 1994 to 1998 and then emigrated to Canada in 2001 (some newspapers reported in 2004) and obtained Canadian citizenship in 2006 and is also married to his wife named Anna.
Vince Lee was in the place of his seat in the first door and stood at Ericsson station before checking them and returning passengers to their seats did not focus on Phineas's place, but walked down the corridor of the door and glanced at each passenger as if looking for someone specific that he got to Tim and sat down next to him, as if he had found the ideal, and Tim slept and her life fell asleep again, at

which time the driver began to calm the lighting so that people could sleep, but the passengers who were next to Tim and Lee, noticed strange behavior on me emanating from him as he began to shake his head from a nervous orgasm and mutter indistinct words, as in the case of epilepsy, which led to fear in the hearts of passengers next to him.

Exactly at eight o'clock in the evening I took out a knife from my pocket, a large stabbing from behind Tim brutally stabbed with a knife to varying degrees in the throat and chest, causing panic and fear among the passengers and accepting the conflict in hysterics, ordered the driver to stop, but he would not have stood him on the highway , meanwhile Tim was brutally stabbed to death after the bedroom, panicked and tried to escape and jump out of the net, but he did not listen, so that he could separate one from the driver and all passengers, he could help Tim, who had long been trying to escape. after several tries I was able to run, but collapsed to the floor by the door, it was a great opportunity for Vince to accept his appeal to Link's all-out 160 punches.

Tim McLean's Mysterious Issue
The door of the incident is closed
Meanwhile, the door was completely devoid of passengers, except for me and Tim, who turned the gap into full of holes, the faster the driver closed the door, the faster the passenger was outside, in case of hysteria and panic, and what would one of them do something with Tim, while there was a big truck, the driver was driving to the bus stop in the same way, when I felt that something abnormal was happening, and when I was offered a story, it was the driver's door that tried to attack, and one of the passengers on me saved the rest of Tim, they brought a piece of iron, significantly increased the calls for the others and walked along the first corridor and tried to threaten him, but he did not pay attention to them and their eyes filled with anger and horror in them, he said to cut off Tim's head, took the looms at three men Quickly leading them out the door and

closing it again from the outside, I tried to run away from the others, but he did not listen to his commands.

Beach came, Canadian company, incident but they arrived too late and are trying to control the bus by the police, the weird thing is that they have been around for five hours, refusing to attack me, they probably expected it to completely calm the culprit, especially after how you make sure Tim is dead and point his head on the track that I had.

At the same time, I looked at Tim's belly flesh slicing and chopping and eating them brutally, and he kept repeating the phrase: ((I must stay at the door forever)), and took him eating parts of his liver and kidney, and most of his hand , Lee tried to escape again led by the door, but it failed again grabbed the knife and began to crack the window glass to escape here the police come they call him arrester electric and restrained by iron and go to the police station and went to the police to the bus address of the place crimes they came here to be with them found pieces of Tim, they were all over the place, and later they found his ear and nose in my pocket.

Tim McLean's Mysterious Issue
Maclean's mother carried the image of the deceased's son
It was actually a forty-year-old man who started an investigation with me who made excuses to do this: "I heard the voice of the Lord telling him that MacLaine must follow Satan to kill him" I said that God began to speak to him since 2004, and after checking me by psychologist Stanley Rin, it turns out that he suffers from schizophrenia with a sharp gesture, he is transferred to a psychiatric hospital for a while, but was released in 2015 after they were convinced that he was not a danger to society and put him under surveillance. and be sure to eat his medicine at his own apartment in Winnipeg.

A strong objection from McLean's mother, Caroline de Deely, whom I regarded as an escape from my insult to Tim and his family.